W9-COA-311

SAINT PETERSBURG

& Its Environs

Alfa-Colour Art Publishers
Saint Petersburg

2003

Text by MARGARITA ALBEDIL

Translated from the Russian by VALERY FATEYEV

Designed by VITALY VIAZOVSKY

Photographs by VALENTIN BARANOVSKY, DARYA BOBROVA,
LEONID BOGDANOV, VLADIMIR DAVYDOV, PAVEL DEMIDOV,
VLADIMIR DENISOV, PAVEL IVANOV, ALEXANDER KASHNITSKY,
LEONARD KHEIFETS, ROMUALD KIRILLOV, SERGEY KOMPANIYCHENKO,
VLADIMIR MELNIKOV, YURY MOLODKOVETS, VICTOR SAVIK,
GRIGORY SHABLOVSKY, YEVGENY SINIAVER
AND OLEG TRUBSKY

Edited by IRINA DUBROVSKAYA

Computer layout by IRINA SEROVA

Color correction by PETER KRAKOVSKY
AND TATYANA KRAKOVSKAYA

Managing editor NINA GRISHINA

© M. Albedil, 2002: texts
© V. Fateyev, 2002: translation
© V. Viazovsky, 2002: design
© V. Baranovsky, D. Bobrova, L. Bogdanov, V. Davydov,
P. Demidov, V. Denisov, P. Ivanov, A. Kashnitsky, L. Kheifets,
R. Kirillov, S. Kompaniychenko, V. Melnikov, Yu. Molodkovets, V. Savik,
G. Shablovsky, Ye. Siniaver, O. Trubsky, 2002: photographs
© Alfa-Colour Art Publishers, St Petersburg, 2002
Colour-separated films produced by the Goland Company

ISBN 5-900958-57-0

eter the Great is a colossal phenomenon in Russian history with no other figure of a similar stature. His age, from the late seventeenth century through the first quarter of the eighteenth, was the era of great achievements and brilliant military victories, the time when Russia joined the European family of peoples. Perhaps there was not a single sphere in the country's life that Peter would not change by his iron will according to European models. "He was your god, Russia!" exclaimed the poet Mikhail Lomonosov in his ode devoted to the Emperor. Peter the Great introduced new forms of governing the country, put in order church affairs, established the Academy of Sciences and founded the first Russian museum – the *Kunstkammer*. He put up large new factories and plants, improved the tax system, introduced more perfect methods in agriculture and horticulture, built new roads, organized trade and postal communication. Many of his reforms have become an essential part of our very being so that now we cannot imagine ourselves living in a different way. It is from Peter's age on that we begin our calendar year in January basing our chronology on the birth of Christ. We read books written in the language innovated by the efforts of Peter the Great, and we are indebted to him even for the typeface used in these books. It was in the

Portrait of Peter the Great
Lacquered miniature. 18th century

time of Peter the Great that the first Russian newspapers, secular schools and secular books appeared. Wine-making, chemists' shops, military hospitals, medicines – we owe all these innovations to the indomitable activities of Peter the Great.

The poet Alexander Pushkin wrote that "Russia entered Europe during the age of Peter the Great as a ship moving down its building slips – accompanied by the striking of axes and the thunder of cannon." The focus of this activity was St Petersburg, the new capital of Russia and "a window onto Europe".

Peter the Great. *Painting by Valentin Serov. 1907*

Perspective View Upstream the Neva from the Admiralty and the Academy of Arts
Engraving by Yefim Vinogradov after a drawing by Mikhail Makhayev. 1749

hree hundred years ago, during the age of Peter the Great, nobody thought about the brilliant grandeur of the capital city on "moss-grown, boggy shores", as Pushkin put it. This territory, then called Ingermanland or Ingria, with the mixed Finnish, Swedish and Izhora population, was ceded to Sweden according to the Stolbovo Treaty of 1617, although it had been part of the Vodsky *piatina* (district) of the Novgorod Principality before. Ingria blocked Muscovy's access to the sea and a war against Sweden was imminent. At the beginning of the eighteenth century the lands around the Neva turned out to be the stage of the prolonged Russo-Swedish conflict known as the Northern War. It was then, to an accompaniment of cannon fire, in gunpowder smoke, that the future capital of Peter's renovated Russia was born.

The course of events was rapid. On 1 May 1703 the Swedish fortress Nyenskans on the right bank of the Neva surrendered, but the Swedish fleet still threateningly loomed in the distance. It was necessary to control the delta of the Neva and the Tsar made up his mind to build a fortress on an islet located in the widest part of the river where it divides into two branches. The islet was called Hare Island by the Finns and Merry Island by the Swedes. On 16 May 1703 work on the site began: sand-banks were artificially raised above the water level, long piles were driven into the bottom and earthen ramparts were put up. In June, the foundations of a wooden church consecrated to the Apostles Peter and Paul, a predecessor of the present-day SS Peter and Paul Cathedral, were laid down. It was then that the fortress was named Saint Petersburg. Under the protection of the fortress ramparts and cannon construction work on Birch Island (now the Petrograd Side) began. A modest timber house called the Red Chamber or the Original Palace (now the memorial Log Cabin of Peter the Great

on the Petrovskaya Embankment) was erected within three days for the Tsar. Soon the first pontoon bridge, a trading arcade and a landing-stage were built, and the first ship with goods moored there. Thus a new city was born as a fortress and a port in the conditions of the war and it was destined to have a great future. The burgeoning city derived its name from the fortress and became the embodiment of the reforms introduced into Russian life by Peter the Great. At first St Petersburg grew in a haphazard way and its future wholly depended on the outcome of the Northern War. In the Battle of Poltava, which took place on 27 June 1709, the Russian troops dealt a crushing blow to the Swedish army. This crucial victory became a new "foundation stone" in the construction of the city on the Neva. In 1712 the royal family moved from Moscow to St Petersburg, together with the government collegias or ministries and numerous dignitaries. And although there was no official decree about the shift of the capital, the new city became the centre of life in the Russian State. The Tsar-Reformer built his favourite "paradise" with a wide sweep and passion, inviting architects from Holland, France and Germany. Peter's ideal was Amsterdam – an accurate, businesslike city that charmed him during his travel abroad. The stone St Petersburg was to replace the wooden Moscow and to win fame as the new Rome, and that is why Peter made the coat-of-arms of his new capital similar to that of the Vatican.

Peter the Great died in 1725 and towards the end of his reign St Petersburg ranked with the largest cities in Russia – one eighth of the entire urban population of the state lived in the northern capital. After the death of the first Russian emperor fate seemed to play with the throne entrusting the crown now to an unstable teenager, now to a child and now to a woman – the latter had never occurred in Russian history before. The appearance of the capital changed in the course of time. Founded as a fortress, port and wharf, St Petersburg

Portrait of Catherine the Great
Painting by Stefano Torelli. 1762

gradually began to develop into a magnificent city of majestic palaces and straight streets. Talented architects carried out a large-scale construction work in the city's central areas. The contribution of such architects as Piotr Yeropkin, Mikhail Zemtsov and Ivan Korobov was especially significant. They mastered the experience of the first St Petersburg architects – Domenico Trezzini, Jean-Baptiste Le Blond, Giovanni Mario Fontana and Georg Johann Mattarnovi, with whom the style of the early Petrine Baroque is usually identified, and contin-

ued along the same lines. The early Baroque style was replaced by the mature Baroque of the 1740s–1760s, with Francesco Bartolomeo Rastrelli as its leading master. The inexhaustible talent of this exuberant Italian flowered during the reign of Empress Elizabeth Petrovna, Peter's daughter. The most significant of Rastrelli's creations, the Winter Palace, is a highlight in the centre of the city to this day.

Further changes in the predominant architectural style as well as in the entire mode of life and politics in the capital, were connected with Catherine the Great. The architects Antonio Rinaldi, Jean-Baptiste Vallin de la Mothe, Alexander Kokorinov and Yury Velten still worked at the junction of the two stylistic eras, but soon the true classicists – Ivan Starov, Charles Cameron, Giacomo Quarenghi and others – ousted them. Many superb palaces were built in those days, and not only in the capital, but in suburbs too – at Peterhof, Tsarskoye Selo, Oranienbaum and Gatchina. The royal suburban palaces surrounded the city like a precious necklace from the age of Peter the Great. Each of the suburban residences had the distinctive features of its own – the seaside Peterhof glistened in the iridescent jets of its fountains; the magnificent new royal residence, Tsarskoye Selo, was notable for its luxury; the elegant Oranienbaum charmed by its Chinese exoticism; the mysterious Gatchina delighted by its romantic atmosphere evoking reminiscences of the Middle Ages. One more suburban residence, Pavlovsk, which emerged in the latter half of Catherine the Great's reign, was remarkable for its poetic landscape park. The most brilliant monument to Catherine's reign is the Hermitage Museum, a treasure-house of unique masterpieces of world art for which magnificent buildings were erected next to the Winter Palace.

The Marble Bridge in the Catherine Park
Watercolour by G. Sergeyev. Second half of the 18th century

In the nineteenth century St Petersburg already graced the banks of the Neva as an embodiment of Peter's dream of "a foothold gaining upon this coast," as Pushkin expressed it. Emperor Alexander I, the grandson of Catherine the Great, who ascended the throne at the beginning of the century, followed in the footsteps of his most august grandmother both in political affairs and in architecture. Inspired by the ideas of High Classicism, the architects of his time created building complexes unseen anywhere in the world. One of them was the ensemble of the Spit of Vasilyevsky Island began by Giacomo Quarenghi and finished by Jean-François Thomas de Thomon. A recognized leader in the construction of large-scale urban complexes was Carlo Rossi, who created within a brief period the superb Palace Square and some other central areas. At the same time Andreyan Zakharov rebuilt Korobov's Admiralty, transforming the glacis in front of it into a boulevard that became a fashionable place of promenades. Andrei Voronikhin built the beautiful Kazan Cathedral enriching Nevsky Prospekt with a new magnificent square.

The victorious War of 1812 against Napoleon Bonaparte further strengthened the position of Russia and towards the middle of the nineteenth century it gained a prominent place among the European states. St Petersburg became one of the largest cities in the world, which "sprung out the dark of mire and wood" all of a sudden. The northern capital admired its guests not only by the miracle of its creation in so brief a time, but by its incomparable majesty and beauty as well. The city was adorned with fine palaces, the Neva was clad with granite, bridges spanned the city's rivers and canals, and green gardens and parks were laid out on its numerous islands. The city grew in an original way following its own laws, so that foreign influences that had left a great imprint on its appearance harmoniously blended with the distinctively Russian features of design and construction. St Petersburg began to decorate itself with triumphal monuments and memorials testifying to the great deeds of Russia's soldiers. The city acquired a gorgeous imperial look. The majestic structures by Vasily Stasov, Avraam Melnikov and other architects added to the city's regal splendour and variety. The thirty years of Nicholas I's reign were especially remarkable architecturally for the creation of such masterpieces as St Isaac's' Cathedral and the Alexander Column by Auguste de Montferrand. The first half of the nineteenth century witnessed the flowering of Russian sculpture. The culminating accomplishments of this fruitful period were the beautiful works by the sculptors Vasily Demuth-

Nevsky Prospekt. *Watercolour by Victor Sadovnikov. 1840s*

*The inauguration of the State Duma
on 27 April 1906. Photograph*

Malinovsky and Stepan Pimenov, which decorated the architectural masterpieces of Carlo Rossi and Vasily Stasov.

From the middle of the nineteenth century onwards, the new capitalist features increasingly pushed out the formerly predominant classical elements. The appearance of houses and streets grew more and more variegated. Eclectic features began to change the architectural appearance of the city. Sometimes different shapes and styles of bygone eras could be combined even in a single building. The architecture of the period was influenced by the aesthetics of Romanticism and interest in the secrets of the human soul, but at the same time the spirit of practical benefit began to dominate St Petersburg society. Most of new buildings were tenement houses with rooms and flats to be lent for temporary living. Architecture was getting, in the words of Nikolai Gogol, a capricious person: now Egyptian motifs, now Chinoiserie, and now mock-Gothic elements filtered into it. The Russo-Byzantine trend, which corresponded to the official ideology of Nicholas I, became fashionable. One of the first adherents of stylization in St Petersburg was Alexander Briullov. The nobility especially liked the work of Andrei Stakenschneider, who built the Mariinsky, Beloselsky-Belozersky, Nicholas and New Michael Palaces. It was in this period that the first permanent bridge across the Neva, the Nicholas (now Lieutenant Schmidt) Bridge was built, the Mariinsky Theatre began to work and the Russian Museum was established. The end of the century saw a real construction boom in the city. The historical centre, that took its final shape by that time, did not suffer from radical alterations – housing construction was carried out mainly

Portrait of Emperor Nicholas II
Painting by Nikolai Kuznetsov. 1915–16

on the outskirts of the city. New types of buildings: railway stations, markets and industrial enterprises – began to emerge. The last major architectural style in the late nineteenth century was Art Nouveau with its elegant and whimsically curving lines, elaborate rhythm of doorways and windows, balconies and oriels, elegant combinations of colour spots and play on various textures. The architect Fiodor Lidval is thought to be the most prominent representative of the Northern Art Nouveau. The main street of the Petrograd Side, Kamennostrovsky Prospekt, begins with the architect's programmatic work, a tenement house owned by his mother I. B. Lidval. One of the first urban ensembles of the twentieth century, it exerted a significant influence on contemporary architects. Another prominent project by Lidval was the well-known building of the Astoria Hotel.

Nevsky Prospekt. Photograph. 1900s

At the beginning of the twentieth century the "brilliant St Petersburg" was the flourishing capital of the Russian Empire, famous not only for its resplendent palaces, but also for its museums, theatres, concert halls and churches. It was, however, the time of incessant trials and tribulations. In February 1913 the tercentennial of the Romanov Dynasty was celebrated on a grand scale, but four years later the revolution erased the autocratic royal power. Shortly before, on 9 January 1905, the city witnessed "bloody Sunday" that marked the beginning of the First Russian Revolution. Under the pressure of these events the last Russian Tsar Nicholas II in December of the same year signed regulations for the elections to the 1st State Duma or Parliament. In April 1906 he held a reception for members of the State Duma in the St George Hall (or the Large Throne Room) in the Winter Palace. Sessions of the first four State Dumas took place in the Tauride Palace, and the same building was to become a scene of major revolutionary events.

The First World War, the October Revolution of 1917 and the fratricidal Civil War, which came in a rapid succession, brought threatening changes into the life of the northern capital. It became the scene of epoch-making and tragic events. The destinies of the city and the country as a whole were decided on Znamenskaya Square and Nevsky Prospekt, in Kschessinska's mansion and at Smolny, as well as in other major streets and buildings. In 1918 the new, Bolshevik government took a decision to leave the city for Moscow and the era of St Petersburg as the capital of the state that lasted nearly for two centuries, came to an end.

During the years of the War of 1941–45, known as the Great Patriotic War in Russia, the city withstood a terrible siege for 900 cold and hungry days, with shelling and air-raids, shortage of electricity, the unserviceable water supply system and other disasters. It took enormous efforts after the war to cure the tormented city's numerous wounds – to restore its destroyed palaces, churches and living buildings. In the course of the entire century St Petersburg never ceased to extend its area and embellish itself with new edifices, parks, bridges and works of monumental and decorative art. Large new residential areas grew on the outskirts of the city, but standardization and lack of variety unfortunately impaired this mass-scale construction.

In the twentieth century the name of the city was changed several times. During the war against Germany in 1914 St Petersburg took the Russianized name of Petrograd (or Peter's City). In 1924, after the death of Lenin, leader of the revolution, the city was renamed Leningrad to regain, however, its original historical name in 1991.

oday, St Petersburg is getting ready for the celebration of its 300th jubilee. In the course of its past centuries, the city lived through the brilliant triumphs of imperial grandeur and the terrible dramas of wars and revolutions. The well-known poet Anna Akhmatova called it "The granite city of glory and victories". St Petersburg occupies a distinctive place of its own in Russia: it has become a symbol of Russian culture, science and spiritual development and has no doubts about its future. As Peter the Great, the founder of the city, believed, the past emphasizes the grandeur of the present.

People come to St Petersburg not only for business or to meet their friends and relations. Many of them visit St Petersburg primarily to have a look at what they cannot see anywhere else in the world. The beautiful museum of a city does not leave anybody indifferent. And it is unique indeed – there are few cities in the world which, like St Petersburg, have not grown naturally from an ancient settlement, but have been created by the will of a single man. The northern capital of Russia never fails to delight its numerous visitors by the beauty of its straight streets and ornate squares, by

its charming, even if not very bright, specifically northern colouring, by a special aura reigning it. Enjoying the city's exquisite and varied architecture, strolling along the granite embankments of the full-flooded Neva, everyone can find convincing evidence that St Petersburg is a truly unique and unfathomable city. It is pleasant in any weather and in any season, be it melancholy rainy days, the magic White Nights, the fascinating golden autumn or the exciting time of spring storms. It is justly said that St Petersburg is not merely the city of poets, but is built itself like a poem – with regular stanzas and well-memorized rhymes. Its panoramic views and silhouettes, spires and domes, arches and bridges can be enjoyed like a beautiful piece of poetry. While wandering about the city and thus turning over the pages of its stone chronicle, you can sense the harmony of its living and dead nature and to enjoy the inexhaustible architectural variety of the northern capital. All kinds of monumental and decorative art contribute amply to its beauty. And although the northern capital is sometimes compared to Rome, called the Venice or Palmyra of the North, it has its own unparalleled grace, its own fascination. The soul of the city will readily reveal itself to you if you try to get in touch with it.

The Peter and Paul Fortress. View from above

The Complex of Central Squares

St Petersburg is a many-faceted city fascinating us by its variety. One of its notable features is the group of central squares perceived as a superb large-scale architectural ensemble. The vast water space of the regal Neva well combines with the "suite" of man-made squares adding to the unity of the stone structures. The spaces of Palace Square, Admiralty Square (now the Admiralty and Alexander Park), Decembrists' Square, Stock Exchange Square and the Field of Mars make up a fine necklace in the centre of the northern capital. The architectural patterns of these squares were formed in the course of two centuries and now, linked into a single whole as they are, they do not resemble one another. Carlo Rossi conceived Palace Square as a rival of ancient Roman structures in sweep and grandeur. The majestic and austere buildings around the square glorified the inflexible power of the Empire. They served as a fitting mount for the Winter Palace, the main decoration of the square put up during the age when Russia had just become a recognized European power. The Triumphal Arch linking the two wings of the General Staff building, as well as the Alexander Column, the highest commemorative pillar in the world, make up a majestic memorial to the feat of the Russian people in the War of 1812 against Napoleon Bonaparte. The central square of St Petersburg is the venue of military parades, meetings, demonstrations and popular merry-making.

Panoramic view of Palace Square

Angel crowning the Alexander Column on Palace Square. Sculptor: Boris Orlovsky, 1834

View of the Winter Palace from the Admiralty side.
The Saltykov Entrance. Architect: Bartolomeo Francesco Rastrelli, 1754–62

*Panoramic view of the Hermitage buildings
from the Spit of Vasilyevsky Island*

The Winter Palace, the city's focal point on Palace Square, was the main residence of the imperial dynasty in St Petersburg. The building is so large that it can be held in view as a whole only from the Neva or from the Spit of Vasilyevsky Island. The last monumental structure in the Baroque style, the Winter Palace was erected "for the glory of Russia". The stately edifice we see today is the fifth building on this site. The first one, a small wooden house, was erected opposite the Peter and Paul Fortress for Peter I in 1711–12 after a "model" project by Domenico Trezzini. In 1716–22, Georg Mattarnovi put up the second Winter Palace near the eastern bank of the Winter Canal, at the place of the present-day Hermitage Theatre. It was in this palace that Peter the Great died on 28 January 1725. In 1726–27, Trezzini enlarged this building for Catherine I. In 1731–35, the fourth Winter Palace was put up to a project by Bartolomeo Francesco Rastrelli. The building seemed to be very large for that period, but in the middle of the eighteenth century Empress Elizabeth Petrovna found it too small for her. So in 1754–62 Rastrelli built a new palace.

In 1767–69, Jean-Baptiste Vallin de la Mothe designed the so-called "La Mothe's Pavilion", now known as the Small Hermitage, and in 1770–87, the architect Yury Velten constructed one more palace – the Large Hermitage. The Hermitage Theatre completed the ensemble of buildings connected by hanging arched passageways and covered bridges. Thus, in a little more than two centuries the Winter Palace grew into a huge complex with living apartments, churches, libraries and gardens. It also had a telegraph, an office, a chemist's shop, flats for servicemen and guards, as well as numerous auxiliary premises – a kitchen, a storeroom, a manège, carriage departments and laundries. The palace grew together with the city and beyond its luxurious, truly regal façades the eight generations of the monarchs governed the activities of the Russian Empire. The private apartments of the imperial family were traditionally located in the western section of the palace.

In 1837 a terrible fire devastated the palace with all its magnificent decor, but within a little more than a year the building was reconstructed and regained its former magnificence. Later its interiors were repeatedly redesigned. In 1922, the Winter Palace was handed over to the Hermitage Museum.

The palace is an integral architectural complex, a city within the city. The two-hundred-metre length of its façade determines the dimensions of Palace Square. Rastrelli, whose fantasy was inexhaustible, designed each front of the palace in a different way. The southern façade was to play the role of the principal entrance – the architect conceived a large formal square in front of it that would be later created by Carlo Rossi.

*The Main (Ambassadors' or Jordan)
Staircase of the Winter Palace
Architects: Bartolomeo Francesco
Rastrelli, 1762; Vasily Stasov, 1838*

When Empress Catherine the Great became the owner of the Winter Palace in the summer of 1762, she arranged in its several rooms a *hermitage*, or a place of retreat. This name was used in the eighteenth century to denote small pavilions in court parks, where one could rest in silence and solitude. The rooms in the palace chosen to imitate this fashionable French invention were decorated with paintings, pieces of sculpture and other art objects. In 1764, 225 paintings were brought to the Empress's Hermitage and from that time onwards works of art were purchased for it one after another. The most valuable acquisition throughout the history of the Hermitage is thought to be the famous Crozat collection purchased in Paris in 1772 through the intermediacy of the well-known French Enlightener Denis Diderot. This collection included more than 400 first-rate paintings including masterpieces by Raphael, Titian and Rembrandt. The Hermitage grew to become a well-known museum and the year 1764 is taken to be the date of its foundation.

Imperial carriages used to come to the main entrance facing Palace Square and on passing through it the owners and guests of the palace found themselves on the southern Jordan (or Ambassadors') Staircase glistening with lavish gilt decoration. In the eighteenth century this staircase was known as the Ambassadors' Staircase, as envoys coming for receptions entered the palace through it. Later it was named the Jordan Staircase because the religious procession used to descend it during the celebration of Epiphany Day on the Neva, in imitation of the Baptism in the Jordan River.

Portrait of Empress
Catherine the Great
*Painting by Fiodor Rokotov.
Late 18th century*

*The Great Carriage for the coronation ceremony. France.
First quarter of the 18th century*

The Hermitage. The St George Hall (Large Throne Room).
Architects: Giacomo Quarenghi, 1795; Vasily Stasov, Nikolai Yefimov, 1837–42

The Hermitage. The Malachite Drawing-Room. Architect: Alexander Briullov, 1839

or a long time only guests of the royal family, people of exalted rank, could enjoy the Hermitage treasures. It was only in 1852, with the inauguration of the New Hermitage, then called the Public Museum, that an access to the art collection became freer. In 1917, after the October Revolution, the Hermitage and the Winter Palace were declared a state museum. Nowadays each visitor to the museum is allowed to view the state rooms of the palace, in which the ceremonial *entrées* of the imperial family used to take place, and to enjoy the beauty of their treasures.

The first owner of the renovated Winter Palace, Catherine the Great, resigned herself to its Baroque outer appearance, but expressed a desire to change the inner decor in the spirit of restrained Classicism. The Empress entrusted the most important part of work to Giacomo Quarenghi. By 1795 he had finished the columns and walls of the St George Hall or Large Throne Room with Carrara marble. This magnificent state room was intended for official ceremonies and receptions. It contained the canopied imperial throne with the coat-of-arms bearing a representation of the victorious St George as the patron of Muscovy – hence the name of the hall. Later a marble relief devoted to the same subject was placed over the throne. The hall suffered during the conflagration of 1837, but the architects Vasily Stasov and Nikolai Yefimov, who designed it anew, made the interior one of the best examples of Russian Classicism. The throne place has been completely restored recently.

The Malachite Room, the decor of which became a model for the decoration of palatial drawing-rooms in the middle of the nineteenth century, produced an indelible impression on its contemporaries. It served as the main drawing-room in the apartments of Alexandra Fiodorovna, the eldest daughter of King Frederick William of Prussia and Nicholas I's wife. It was also here, in the Malachite Room, that a session of the Provisional Government was being held in October 1917 when a volley fired from the cruiser *Aurora* signalled the beginning of the Bolshevik revolution. Originally designed by Auguste de Montferrand, the room was restored after the fire of 1837 by Alexander Briullov. The architect used for the new decor malachite delivered by Demidov, a wealthy owner of mines in the Urals. The columns, pilasters and fireplaces of the room were adorned with thin plaques of malachite in the so-called "Russian technique".

The Hermitage. The Hall of Peter the Great. Architects: Auguste de Montferrand, 1833; Vasily Stasov, 1839

any rooms of the Hermitage Museum built by talented master craftsmen to designs by outstanding architects are superb examples of Russian art. One of them is the Peter Hall (Small Throne Room) conceived as a memorial room. Decorated by Auguste de Montferrand in 1833 in the spirit of Late Classicism, it was re-created after the fire by Vasily Stasov to its former appearance. The design of the hall — the stucco ornament, the ceiling painting, the frieze on the walls including Peter's Latin monogram, the double-headed eagles and crowns — perfectly corresponds to its use. On the walls, at the top, are historical paintings by the Italian artists Barnaba Medici and Pietro Scotti. The pictures feature the famous victorious battles of Poltava and Lesnaya during the Northern War against Sweden. In the depth of a niche between the jasper columns hangs the allegorical canvas *Peter the Great with the Goddess Minerva* by the Venetian painter Jacopo Amiconi. Under the painting stands the imperial throne made in England by Nicholas Clausen in 1731

for the Russian Empress Anna Ioannovna. Most of objects marked by a rare taste and mastery were produced by the best St Petersburg craftsmen in the eighteenth century.

Of particular interest is also the interior of the Golden Room — a dazzling large corner room once occupied by Grand Duchess Maria Alexandrovna. Illuminated from large windows on bright days, it looks light and airy. The overall character of its luxurious decor, executed by the architect Alexander Briullov, echoes in some way the Malachite Drawing-Room, which was also known as the "golden" one in the nineteenth century. The room is provided with gilt furniture modelled on sumptuous Baroque examples by Andrei Stakenschneider. Nowadays, the Golden Drawing-Room houses a large collection of carved gems, which rivals the most brilliant assemblages of this kind in the world. The fine cameos and intaglios displayed in this lavishly decorated interior were carved in cornelian, onyx, amethyst and other semiprecious stones by Western European master craftsmen. The origins of this representative collection go back to Catherine the Great who was fond of carved gems.

The Winter Palace. The Golden Drawing-Room. Architects: Alexander Briullov, 1839; Victor Schreiber, 1860

The Small Hermitage. The Pavilion Hall. Architect: Andrei Stakenschneider, 1850–58
This ornate hall decorated in an oriental style is used to display magnificent examples of Italian and Russian mosaics.

The Peacock Clock. By James Cox. 18th century
The clock is reminiscent of a fairy-tale garden – its dial is in the cap
of the large mushroom, while the complex mechanism is concealed under the bill.

The Old Hermitage. The Leonardo da Vinci Room
Architects: Giacomo Quarenghi, 1805–07; Andrei Stakenschneider, 1858

The Department of Western European Art is the earliest in the Hermitage. Works by Western European masters became the first accessions that made up the core of the future art collections of the now famous museum. There were some first-rate examples of High Renaissance art. The art collections of Catherine the Great were preserved in the hall situated near the end of the long suite of rooms created by Yury Velten in the Old Hermitage. These interiors were not designed for a display of paintings and works of art were arranged on the walls of the palace with no system at all, just to gladden the eye. The interior acquired its present-day appearance in 1858, when the architect Andrei Stakenschneider redecorated the entire enfilade.

Today, the room is used to display the paintings by Leonardo da Vinci. The celebrated Italian master practiced various kinds of art, but was not very prolific as a painter and, besides, more than a half of his creations disappeared. Two of his few authentic surviving paintings, *The Madonna with a Flower* and *The Madonna and Child*, grace this beautiful interior.

Leonardo da Vinci
The Madonna and Child ("The Litta Madonna"). *Ca 1490*

Francisco de Surbarán
The Childhood of the Madonna. *Ca 1600*

he Hermitage is considered to be the world's largest picture gallery. Its rich collections displayed in more than one hundred halls and rooms, as well as kept in the stocks amount to about 8,000 paintings of different Western European schools from the late Medieval Ages to the present day. One can enjoy here works by nearly all outstanding masters of Western Europe. A gem of these holdings is the superb collection of Spanish painting, perhaps the best outside Spain. It boasts works by all the great Spanish artists – El Greco, Ribera, Surbarán, Velázquez, Murillo and Goya. Its most valuable part consists of paintings by the foremost artists of the eighteenth century, which is reckoned to be the "Golden Age" of Spanish national culture.

Visitors to the museum are invariably attracted to the Hermitage's collection of Dutch painting, also one of the most representative in the world. Its highlight is an outstanding assemblage of paintings by the great Rembrandt Harmensz van Rijn (1606–1669) complemented by his no less superb graphic works. Dutch paintings appeared in St Petersburg during the age of Peter the Great, long before the establishment of the Hermitage Museum. Rembrandt was one of the Tsar's favourite painters.

Rembrandt Harmensz van Rijn. The Return of the Prodigal Son. *1668–69*

In 1842–51, the building of the New Hermitage was put up to a design by the German architect Leo von Klenze. It continued the Winter Palace and was to function both as a museum of art and part of the imperial premises. This explains the luxurious decor and furnishings of the rooms, unusual for a museum. The Russian tsars used to have merry masked balls and festive dinners here, and this was not good for works of art. The first floor of the palace was intended for a display of paintings and therefore the ceilings in the large skylight rooms were glazed. And although the glazed space is not large and lighting is still insufficient owing to short northern daytime, the very idea to illuminate paintings by a diffused light from above was an innovatory one and was an evidence of a careful attitude to the museum. The ceilings around the glazed sections were decorated with sumptuous moulded and gilt ornaments on a blue ground. This pattern perfectly combined with the deep dark red shade of the walls hung with paintings. The rooms were richly decorated: they were provided with gilt furniture produced specially for these interiors, which were also adorned with huge vases and tables of different coloured stones. Particularly notable among various items of decoration are vases, standard lamps, table-tops and other articles of Urals malachite, Badakhshan lapis lazuli, Korgon porphyry and rhodonite executed in the so-called "Russian technique" and richly embellished with ormolu. These decorative objects are the best examples of Russian stone-carving.

But despite its luxury, the decor of the rooms does not distract visitors from viewing the paintings. The armchairs and sofas are arranged so that resting people are able to continue to enjoy the pictures. Nowadays the skylight rooms house Italian and Spanish painting of the seventeenth and eighteenth centuries.

Judith by Giorgione ranks with masterpieces of the Venetian School. The painting revives the heroic subject of a biblical legend: the beautiful Judith penetrated into the tent of the Assyrian leader Holophernes, charmed and then decapitated him to make the enemy's army retreat. The general trend of Giorgione's work exerted a major influence on the painters of the Venetian School and was developed by his pupil Titian, whose works can also be found in the Hermitage.

Giorgione. Judith. *Ca 1504*

The New Hermitage. The Large Italian Skylight Room. Architect: Leo von Klenze, 1840s

Auguste Rodin. Eternal Spring. *After 1884*

The Hermitage collection contains nine works by Auguste Rodin
including *Romeo and Juliet, Cupid and Psyche* and *A Sinner.*

The Rooms of Eighteenth-Century French Art

he Hermitage collection of French painting is the second best in the world after the Louvre in terms of the quantity and quality of its exhibits. An idea of predominant tastes in eighteenth-century France can be received from the works of Antoine Watteau, one of the best artists of his time, as well as from paintings by François Boucher and sculptural pieces by Etienne Maurice Falconet and Jean Houdon. Auguste Rodin, the best sculptor of the late nineteenth and early twentieth centuries, also represented in the Hermitage, repudiated the conventional precepts of academic art and made a decisive step towards the revival of realist sculpture. He could perfectly play on the contrast of light, plastic bodies and the ponderous quality of an angular block of stone.

Etienne Maurice Falconet. Cupid Menacing with His Finger. *1758*

Pablo Picasso. Guitar and Violin. *1913*

The Hermitage collection of works by Pablo Picasso, one of the founders of Cubism in France, contains about forty pieces and belongs to the early period of his work covering some fifteen years. It is famous for a number of excellent pieces such as *The Absinthe Drinker, The Visit (Two Sisters)* and others.

*T*he most remarkable section of French art in the Hermitage is the collection of Impressionist paintings including works by Claude Monet, Auguste Renoir, Edgar Degas, Camille Pissarro, Paul Cézanne and other great masters. Their works are especially notable for the specific pictorial devices that were a result of a new world perception. It was the Impressionist group that "opened" this aspect of the world not noticed by artists before them, and turned to the changing and transitory in it expressing their personal impressions and moods and emphazing the value of fleeting moments.

The work of Henri Matisse, one of the leading masters of world painting, is represented in the Hermitage by a collection of about forty canvases. It contains still lifes, decorative panels, portraits and genre scenes. Matisse was the most significant artist of the Fauve group of painters. His point of departure was the thesis that verisimilitude was not truth. The artist keenly felt his material and a correlation of a drawing with the format of the paper and attached great significance to colour.

Kees van Dongen. The Red Dancer. *1907*

Henri Matisse. The Dance. *1910*

Vincent van Gogh
Cottages. *1890*

◀ *Paul Gauguin*
Pastorales tahitiennes. *1893*

Wassily Kandinsky. Winter. *1909*

Van Gogh and Gauguin, who evolved their own distinctive methods in painting, occupy a place apart next to the galaxy of the Impressionists. Paintings by Gauguin in the Hermitage collection belong to the period when the artist fled from stifling civilization to Tahiti Island and spent the rest of his life on islands in the Pacific trying to find harmony and calm there. *Pastorales tahitiennes (Tahitian Pastorals)* is one of the best works by Gauguin. The artist himself said that he wanted to convey in his paintings "the accord of human life with the life of animals and plants" and "to give more place to the voice of the earth".

Similarly restless was the life of Gauguin's friend Vincent Van Gogh. Among his works in the Hermitage is the canvas *Cottages* painted during the year of the artist's death. It gives some idea of Van Gogh's last period. Infatuated with Oriental art, especially with the Japanese woodcut, he perceived the world "with Japanese eyes". His naturalness was a result of his utmost truthfulness. Van Gogh said about himself that he stands in art "precisely where he is in life itself". His methods later exerted a significant influence on the work of the European Expressionists. The Hermitage also owns a number of works by Wassily Kandinsky, the initiator of Abstract Expressionism and one of the foremost artists of the twentieth century.

A single tour of the rooms and halls of the Hermitage will allow you just to form a general idea of the character and scale of Russia's largest museum, its history, the architectural splendour of its halls and rooms and the endless variety of the collections displayed in them. The interiors of the Winter Palace and other Hermitage buildings created by the outstanding master craftsmen — builders, stonecarvers, moulders and guilders — are magnificent examples of Russian art in their own right. Besides permanent displays, the Hermitage arranges many temporal exhibitions, which are now held in the recently opened rooms of the General Staff building.

The New Hermitage. Portico with Atlantes.
Architect: Leo von Klenze, sculptor: Alexander Terebenev, 1848

The building of the Main Admiralty. Architects: Ivan Korobov, 1728–35;
Andreyan Zakharov, sculptors: Ivan Terebenev, Feodosy Shchedrin, 1806–23

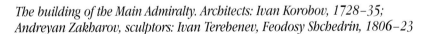

*T*he Admiralty is an architectural masterpiece and a symbol of the northern capital. Its spire can be seen from a long distance and all the principal thoroughfares of the city, including Nevsky Prospekt, are focused on it. The contemporary building of the Admiralty is the third one. The first Admiralty, founded by Peter the Great as a shipyard and citadel, was rebuilt by Ivan Korobov in the 1730s. In 1806–23 a new stately edifice based on Korobov's building was erected in the Empire style to a design by Andreyan Zakharov. The three sides of the Admiralty overlook three major areas in the centre of the city – Palace, St Isaac's and Decembrists' Squares and serve as important formative elements in their outlines. Thanks to pavilions, arches and sculptural decorations the Admiralty produces a different impression from various sides.

Monument to Emperor Nicholas I. Architect: Auguste de Montferrand,
sculptors: Peter Klodt, Robert Salemann, Nikolai Ramazanov, 1856–59

St Isaac's Square with the monument to Nicholas I and the Astoria Hotel. Architect: Fiodor Lidval, 1908–12

t is impossible to imagine St Petersburg without its monuments, memorials, statues and other examples of urban sculpture. One of the most notable among them is the monument to Nicholas I erected on St Isaac's Square to a project by Auguste de Montferrand in 1856–59. The sculptor Peter Klodt designed the six-metre bronze equestrian statue of the Emperor so that it rests only on two points of support, which is extremely rare with monuments of this kind. The Tsar, in the tightly fitted uniform of an officer of the Horse Guards Regiment, seems to prance on the drilling ground before the formed up lines of the regiment. On the four sides of the many-tiered pedestal made of Finnish granite, Serdobolye stone, Shoksha porphyry and Carrara marble are surmounted the allegorical figures of Wisdom, Power, Justice and Faith, in which Nicholas I's contemporaries recognized the features of his consort and three daughters. The large images in high relief illustrate episodes of his reign and the most complimentary opinions about the monarch. The overall silhouette and scale of the monument perfectly harmonizes with the space of the square.

The shaping of the present-day appearance of St Isaac's Square was completed only in the 1910s when the German architect Peter Behrens erected the building of the German embassy and Fiodor Lidval completed in 1912 the construction of the Astoria Hotel on the opposite side of the square. The leading master of the Northern Art Nouveau succeeded in blending innovatory features with an adherence to the St Petersburg traditions. Art Nouveau elements are well combined with Classical details in the architectural design and interior decor of this elegant building. Fiodor Lidval succeeded in creating an illusion of a lower height for the six-storeyed building with an attic, too high for the square. He attained that by including into his design a powerful cornice over the last but one, fifth storey; while the smoothly tapering angle enabled him to integrate the new edifice with the panorama of the square and to shape the entry to it from Large Morskaya Street.

The Astoria Hotel welcomed its first residents in 1912 and from the first years of its existence won a reputation of the most convenient and comfortable hotel in the northern capital on a par with the best foreign hotels. It is favourably located in the central part of the city, not far from the Neva, and near administrative and business quarters, amidst superb architectural landmarks. It is convenient both for tourists and businessmen coming to establish commercial contacts. Thousands of guests to the city have a good memory about this hotel after their visits to the city.

St Isaac's Cathedral. The Resurrection. *Relief
on the northern pediment. Sculptor: Philippe Lemaire, 1842–44*

S t Isaac's functions both as a church and a memorial museum. Its golden dome can be seen from the Gulf of Finland and the observation deck of the cathedral affords a fine all-round view of the city. The chief creation of Auguste de Montferrand, the cathedral completed the age of Russian Classicism and became the dominant feature of the central squares of St Petersburg and one of its symbols. Originally the Church of St Isaac of Dalmatia, a wooden and ungainly one, was erected on the Admiralty Meadow in 1707. Peter wanted to perpetuate by its erection his birthday that coincided with the church feast of St Isaac – 30 May. In 1717–27, approximately on the site where the Bronze Horseman stands, a stone church was built. The present-day cathedral was built on the site of the third church. The construction of the latter began in 1768 by Antonio Rinaldi and finished in 1802 by Vinzenzo Brenna, but the church proved to be a failure. Montferrand's successful version was under construction within forty years, from 1818 to 1858, many intervals and alterations in the project. The building stands on tarred piles 6.5 metres long over which a massive foundation of granite blocks and rubbles was laid. The walls faced with Karelian marble were erected after the columns of the porticoes had been set up. Outside the cathedral was lavishly embellished with sculpture that transformed it into the largest and probably unique complex of this kind in European art of the nineteenth century.

St Isaac's Cathedral in Scaffolding. *1845. Lithograph from a drawing by Auguste de Montferrand*

Contemporaries were especially impressed by the process of unloading and installing the columns for St Isaac's porticoes. The entire imperial family and numerous guests gathered to see the setting up of the first column on 20 March 1828. In total, the building has 112 columns.

St Isaac's Cathedral. The nave. The main iconostasis. Painters: Timoleon Neff,
Fiodor Briullov, Semion Zhivago and others; sculptor: Peter Klodt

St Isaac's Cathedral. The drum of the main dome. Painter: Karl Briullov.
Statues of angels. Sculptors: Ivan Vitali, Robert Salemann, V. Beliayev

Soon after the consecration of St Isaac's Cathedral a contemporary wrote: "The harmony of the outer and inner decor, the elegance and beauty of the whole and details, the luxury and at the same time a majestic beauty of the entire church make this cathedral one of the most splendid buildings in our city." More than forty kinds of precious stones, including malachite, lapis lazuli, porphyry, jasper and marbles of various shades, were used in its inner decor. One can see in the cathedral numerous works of painting and mosaics by Karl Briullov, Fiodor Bruni, Piotr Basin, Vasily Shebuyev and other talented Russian artists. The cathedral is adorned with numerous pieces of sculpture by such famous sculptors as Ivan Vitali, Nikolai Pimenov, Peter Klodt and others. The overall area of the mosaic pictures specially created for the cathedral is about 600 square metres. Paintings, mosaics and sculpture, the effective combination of decorative stones and gilding produces a very rich colour range, but they can be perceived as a single whole whith

difficulty – details are better to be seen separately and then they amaze by their perfect shapes and finish.

An indelible impression is produced by the iconostasis of the main chancel adorned with malachite and lapis lazuli columns and with mosaic icons of the patron saints of the Russian tsars during whose reigns all the four versions of the Church of St Isaac of Dalmatia were built. There are also painted icons of the Old Testament Prophets. Over the altar gates is the sculptural group *Christ in Glory*, which is surmounted by the mosaic icon *The Last Supper* created under the influence of the well-known mural by Leonardo da Vinci. The stained-glass set in the window of the main chancel is a unique work of art. Covering an area of about thirty square metres – it is probably the only element of Catholic decor in the Orthodox church.

Also unique and large, but at the same time elegant and light in design, is the dome of the cathedral – the only one of this type not only in Russia but in Europe as well.

The main cathedral of the northern capital and the largest in the city can accommodate up to 14,000 believers.

Decembrists' Square with the monument to Peter the Great and a view of the Neva,
the Academy of Sciences, Kunstkammer and the Peter and Paul Fortress

Decembrists' Square (earlier Senate Square) was named in 1925 in honour of the Russian revolutionaries of noble birth who rebelled in December 1825 against the autocratic rule and serfdom. The western wing of the Admiralty skirts the eastern part of the square, while the buildings of the Senate and the Holy Synod frame it from the west. The Senate and the Holy Synod were at the top of the ruling pyramid in the Russian Empire, the fundamental principles of which were introduced by Peter the Great. Carlo Rossi built two majestic edifices for them in 1829–34 using the houses that had stood in the same place. At the desire of Nicholas I the new buildings were designed so as to match the Admiralty in their dimensions and architectural decor and this resulted in the creation of a splendid architectural complex. Thanks to the arch linking the buildings of the Senate and the Holy Synod, they seem to be a single structure.

In the centre of the square enclosed by the austere classical lines of the Admiralty, Senate and Synod, against the background of the huge St Isaac's, stands a masterpiece of monumental sculpture, the monument to Peter the Great. The monument, unveiled in 1782, is generally known, after Pushkin's apt expression, as the "Bronze Horseman". Catherine, who took a decision to erect this monument, the first in St Petersburg, entrusted the designing of this project to the French sculptor Etienne Maurice Falconet. Falconet's assistant Marie Collot created the emperor's head after a model by Bartolomeo Carlo Rastrelli. The sculptor deviated from the traditional canons and portrayed the Tsar-Reformer not in his full uniform, but wearing simple and loose clothes, and seated on an animal cloth rather than on a rich saddle. Only the laurel wreath and the sword attached to the belt indicate Peter's role as a victorious warrior. The monument suggests how the contemporaries of Catherine the Great, people of the age of the Enlightenment, saw him.

According to Falconet's concept, a pedestal for the monument was to be made of a solid "wild rock". A suitable large boulder was discovered not far from St Petersburg, near Lakhta, where locals called it "Thunder-Stone". The boulder, weighing 1600 tons, was delivered to the square with the help of bronze balls and grooved rails.

Monument to Peter the Great (The Bronze Horseman)
Sculptor: Etienne Maurice Falconet, with a participation of Marie Anne
Collot and Fiodor Gordeyev, architect: Yury Velten, 1766–82

The Naval Cathedral of St Nicholas and the Epiphany.
Architect: Savva Chevakinsky, 1753–62

he "New Holland is a remnant of old St Petersburg surviving between the River Moika and two artificial waterways – the Kriukov and Admiralty Canals. The island owes its name to the canals dug there – the artificial waterways reminded to Peter the Great his favourite Holland. The similarly named shipyard was second to the Admiralty and was used for the construction of small and middle-size sailing ships. It was here that at the dawn of the northern capital the basic part of the galley fleet was built, as were battleships. In the first half of the eighteenth century timber for ships was kept in wooden structures erected by the architect Ivan Korobov. But they soon deteriorated and in 1765 a decision was taken to replace them with stone buildings to a design by Savva Chevakinsky. The construction work progressed slowly and was completed only in the middle of the nineteenth century. The architect Jean-Baptiste Vallin de la Mothe designed the façades of the large brick buildings and created an effective arch over the canal leading from the Moika into the depth of the island. The arch is considered to be "one of the most inspiring architectural whims, surviving from old St Petersburg."

With Savva Chevakinsky is also associated one of the most revered ecclesiastical buildings in St Petersburg – the St Nicholas Cathedral, a unique example of the Elizabethan Baroque. Built in order to "adequately commemorate the glorious deeds of the Russian Navy", it was consecrated to St Nicholas the Miracle-Worker, patron of sailors. A decree "on the construction of a stone church at the Naval Regiment Yard" was signed by Empress Elizabeth in 1752 and the ceremony of the cathedral's consecration took place in 1762 in the presence of Empress Catherine the Great. She presented to the cathedral ten icons featuring the saints on whose church feast-days the Russian Navy defeated the Turkish Fleet. Many generations of Russian sailors reverently attended this cathedral for special festive services and offices of the dead. Services on the occasion of a departure to the sea and a return to the native shores, the start of work on a new ship and its launching are also performed here. The walls of the cathedral witnesed many events associated with the history of the Russian Navy.

The Arch of the "New Holland". Architects: Savva Chevakinsky,
Jean-Baptiste Vallin de la Mothe, 1756–89

The Naval Cathedral of St Nicholas and the Epiphany. Icon: St Nicholas the Miracle-Worker. *17th century*

The slender and elegant four-tiered bell-tower of the St Nicholas Cathedral with a thin spire and exquisite architectural forms reflecting in the smooth water of the Kriukov Canal is one of the most beautiful and romantic corners of the old city.

The cathedral has two storeys, with upper and lower churches. It continued to function throughout the years of Soviet power and therefore its inner decor has survived in a beautiful state. The decor is unique because almost all other examples of the Baroque style in the city were destroyed. The architect Savva Chevakinsky introduced into the design of the façades and interiors some notable features of palatial architecture. He also designed the iconostasis for the upper church. It was carved by a group of craftsmen headed by Ignaty Kanayev, a brilliant master of wood-carving. Icons for the upper and lower iconostases were painted by the then well-known painters, the brothers Mina and Fiodor Kolokolnikov. Semion Zolotoy, one of the best master craftsmen of the period, was responsible for the gilding. The colonnade and the canopy over the chancel are veritable masterpieces of Russian decorative art.

The Cathedral of St Nicholas has become a symbol of St Petersburg and its slender detached bell-tower is a favourite motif with artists.

The bell-tower of the Naval Cathedral of St Nicholas

The Naval Cathedral of St Nicholas. Interior ▶

The Mariinsky Theatre. Architects: Albert Cavos, 1847–59; Victor Schröter, 1883–86

There are more than forty theatres in St Petersburg, and many touring companies also perform in various local "palaces of culture". The first theatre was established in St Petersburg in 1714, in the palace of Natalia Alexeyevna, sister of Peter the Great, and the opera and ballet companies were formed at the court of Empress Anna Ioannovna in the 1730s. Since then opera and ballet performances in the Russian capital have never ceased and St Petersburg ballet has never lost its leading position in world art.

The Mariinsky Theatre of Opera and Ballet situated on Theatre Square is a pride of the city. This square was used for theatrical spectacles since long ago. Carnivals and performances of amateurish troupes took place in the wooden building of the theatre put up in 1765. Seventeen years later Antonio Rinaldi erected on the site of the wooden building a stone theatre, which was known as the Bolshoi Theatre and was the largest of this kind in Europe. Operas, ballets and dramas were performed on its stage. The building was repeatedly reconstructed, burnt down and was built again. In the late nineteenth century, after a new reconstruction, it was used for the Conservatoire, the first high-er musical establishment in Russia. Among its graduates were Piotr Tchaikovsky, Dmitry Shostakovich and other well-known composers and musicians.

Opposite the building of the Conservatoire until the middle of the nineteenth century was located the Imperial Theatre-cum-Circus. Its architecture was based on the type of theatrical building with several tiers of boxes and seats that was evolved in the late eighteenth and early nineteenth centuries. After a fire of 1859 the architect Albert Cavos reconstructed the building and it was handed over to the Mariinsky Theatre, named so in honour of Empress Maria Fiodorovna, wife of Alexander II. The theatre opened in 1860 with a performance of Mikhail Glinka's opera *A Life for the Tsar (Ivan Susanin)*. The best achievements of the Russian ballet and operatic art are associated with this building. Maurice Petipa headed its ballet company for several years. Many outstanding soloists performed on its stage, including such world celebrities as the singers Fiodor Chaliapin and Leonid Sobinov, and the dancers Anna Pavlova, Tatyana Karsavina, Mathilda Kschessinska, Vaclav Nijinsky and Galina Ulanova. The theatre changed its name several times. Today it bears again its original name and remains the company of beautiful performers famous all over the world.

The Nutcracker, *ballet by Piotr Tchaikovsky, staged by Mikhail Chemiakin*

Sadko, *opera by Nikolai Rimsky-Korsakov*

The Yusupov Palace. Architects: Jean-Baptiste Vallin de la Mothe, 1760s;
Andrei Mikhailov II, 1830–38; Hyppolito Monighetti, 1858–59

The Yusupov Palace. Private apartments of Felix Yusupov the Younger. 1916
Architect: Andrei Beloborodov. Display

The Yusupov Palace. The Moorish Drawing-Room.
Architects: Hyppolito Monighetti, 1860s; Alexander Stepanov, 1890s

Not far from Theatre Square, on the left bank of the Moika, is the Yusupov Palace, which houses, from 1925, the Palace of Culture of Educational Workers (Teachers' House). The palace owes its name to the family of Prince Yusupov, one of the richest families in Russia, who were owners of the palace from 1830 to 1917. Although the palace probably does not rival the most beautiful buildings of the city as regards its outward appearance, its interiors, however, are remarkable for a rare grandeur and elegance. The marble Staircase with sphinxes and cupids, the Ballroom with slender columns, elegant drawing-rooms, studies lined with cloth or trimmed with oak, all show that the Yusupovs spared no expense and employed the best master craftsmen. The exotic and exquisite decor of the Moorish Drawing-Room, for example, is a tribute to the vogue of the mid-nineteenth century. The ornate palatial Theatre, previously used for domestic performances, is now employed by the Chamber Musical Theatre. A special suite of rooms was designed to preserve a superb collection of paintings, sculpture, jewellery and decorative art – one of the best private collections in Europe. The palace ranked with the most luxurious buildings in the capital and its Theatre was famous far beyond the city.

Invariably popular with tourists is an exhibition devoted to the conspiracy against Grigory Rasputin, a favourite of the imperial family. It was here, in the Yusupov Palace, that during the night of 17 December 1916 the monarchist conspirators killed Grigory Rasputin and drowned his body in the Moika.

Vasilyevsky Island

The panorama of Vasilyevsky Island with its straight lines of slender architectural monuments and wide water expanses never fails to produce a great impression on those who see it for the first time. Vasilyevsky Island is the southern and largest island in the delta of the Neva: it occupies an area of more than a thousand hectares. In the distant past elks roamed about the island and so its Finnish name was Harvisaari, Elk's Island. It is difficult to trace the origin of the island's Russian name today – whether Vasily was the Novgorodian posadnik (governor) who owned these lands in the fifteenth century or it was the name of some other person. In the middle of the 1710s Peter the Great decided to fashion the island as the centre of the new capital and to make of it the Russian Amsterdam with a network of streets-canals. The plan of the construction work was based on projects by Domenico Trezzini and Jean-Baptiste Le Blond, but none of them was carried out. The geometrically arranged lines of avenues and streets of the island remind us now of Peter's unrealized dream. The wide Neva seems to embrace the Spit of Vasilyevsky Island washing it by two powerful branches – the Large Neva and the Small Neva. The bridges across them link the Spit with the left bank of the Neva and the Petrograd Side. Bolshoi Prospekt, the main street of the island, leads to the sea, to the "maritime gate" of the city – the passenger seaport.

Panoramic view
of Vasilyevsky Island

The Stock Exchange. *Coloured lithograph by Jean Jacottet and Aubrin after a drawing by Joseph Charlemagne. Mid-19th century*

The splendid architectural complex of the Spit of Vasilyevsky Island, a unique ensemble unparalleled in Europe, produces an especially strong impression from the Trinity Bridge and from the Peter and Paul Fortress. The lines of the embankments blend into a grand panorama highlighted by such magnificent buildings as the Hermitage, Admiralty, St Isaac's Cathedral, the Stock Exchange and the Custom-House. To use a musical metaphor, all these landmarks sound together like a majestic symphony with the Spit of Vasilyevsky Island as its crowning chord. The focus of the ensemble is the building of the Stock Exchange reminiscent of a majestic ancient temple. The Rostral Columns – triumphal structures and lighthouses – introduce heroic and romantic notes into the ensemble. The steep descends, stone spheres on pediments, arches and lion masks complete the inimitable architectural entity.

The Spit took its final, present-day appearance not at once. Although it was planned to lay out the main square of the city as early as the reign of Peter the Great, the space lacked unity for a long time. The architect Thomas de Thomon suggested an idea of its complete rearrangement. His project began to be carried out in 1804. The foundation of the Stock Exchange was laid in 1805, in the presence of the Tsar's family, and a celebration to mark this memorable event was organized throughout the city with a festive dinner financed by merchants. The inauguration of the Stock Exchange was postponed owing to the war against Napoleon Bonaparte. The ceremony took place only in 1816. Later, in 1826–32, the project of Giovanni Luchini was used to build the southern and northern warehouses overlooking the Large and Small Neva. In 1829–32 the building of the Custom-House was put up nearby, also to a project by Luchini. Designed in the style of Italian Classicism, it complemented the superb architectural complex of old St Petersburg. Today, the building of the Stock Exchange houses the Central Naval Museum, while the southern Warehouse is used by the Museum of Zoology and the northern one, by academic institutions. The former Custom-House is now occupied by the so-called Pushkin House – the Institute of Russian Literature and the Museum of Literature. The tower of the Custom-House on the bank of the Small Neva seems to echo the tower of the Kunstkammer on the bank of the Large Neva. During inundations the river had flooded the Spit and so the area was filled with earth to raise its level higher above the water. As a result the Spit expanded for a hundred metres into the Neva and a semicircular square in front of the Stock Exchange building was formed.

View of the Spit of Vasilyevsky Island from the Palace Embankment

One of the Rostral Columns on the Spit of Vasilyevsky Island. 1807–10. Architect: Jean-François Thomas de Thomon

The monumental 32-metre-high Rostral Columns, notable for their perfect proportions and fine silhouette, are clearly highlighted against the background of the St Petersburg sky. Erected in 1810 by Thomas de Thomon, they can be seen from afar. The columns are installed on either side of the semicircular square in front of the Stock Exchange building emphasizing its dominating position in the ensemble of the Spit of Vasilyevsky Island and lending a festive air to the entire square.

The columns were erected in imitation of an ancient Roman custom to put up triumphal columns in honour of naval victories and decorate them with rostra – the prows of defeated ships. The best St Petersburg stone carver Samson Sukhanov produced the allegorical figures and the bases of the columns personifying the rivers Volkhov, Neva, Dnieper and Volga after models by the French sculptors Joseph Camberlain and Philippe Thibault. In the period before 1885, when there had been a port near the Spit, the columns also served as lighthouses: the winding stairways inside of them lead to the upper platforms where signal lamps were kept burning. Since 1957, when gas has been supplied to the jets in the bowls, bright torches are lit over the Rostral Columns on festive days.

Allegorical statue of The Neva *at the base of the Rostral Column. Sculptor: Philippe Thibault*

Panoramic view of the University Embankment with the building of the Kunstkammer (view from the left bank of the Neva)
Architects: Georg Johann Mattarnovi, Nikolaus-Friedrich Härbel, Gaetano Chiaveri, 1718–34

There is a sort of St Petersburg's "Latin Quarter" on Vasilyevsky Island. Since the late eighteenth and early nineteenth century many research and educational establishments of the city began to concentrate in this part of the city: the Academy of Sciences and academic institutes, the University, the Academy of Arts, the Mining Institute, etc. It was also in this area, on the University Embankment, that the first Russian museum was located. Peter the Great founded it in 1714 by on the basis of his private collections acquired during his travels to Western Europe. In 1718–34 Mattarnovi built especially for the museum the building of the *Kunstkammer*, or the Cabinet of Curios. Now this is one of a few surviving buildings of the Petrine Baroque. It houses the Peter the Great Museum of Anthropology and Ethnography and the Museum of Mikhail Lomonosov. Next to the Kunstkammer is the building of the Academy of Sciences – a fine example of austere Classicism put up in 1783–87 to a project by Giacomo Quarenghi. There is also one more unique edifice dating from the age of Peter the Great – the building of the Twelve Collegia, or ministries, built according to a project by Domenico Trezzini in 1722–42 for the government of the Russian Empire. Today it houses St Petersburg University. The building stands with its side to the Neva, because Trezzini planned to create a square in front of it when Peter the Great conceived to shift the centre of the newly found capital to Vasilyevsky Island.

The Kunstkammer. The Museum of Mikhail Lomonosov.
The table around which sessions of the first Russian Academicians were held.

The Kunstkammer. The round hall dedicated to the history of the museum's first collections

T here is a prominent building on the University Embankment – the Palace of Alexander Menshikov, Peter the Great's principal associate. The palace is the first large-scale stone structure of Peter's time on Vasilyevsky Island. The island was presented by the Tsar to his favourite, the first Governor-General of St Petersburg and one of the richest men in Russia. Built in a "European manner", according to a project by Domenico Fontana and Johann Georg Schädel, the palace amazed contemporaries by its dimensions and the luxury of its decor. It was the most sumptuous edifice in the northern capital in the first quarter of the eighteenth century. The interiors of the first floor were especially rich in decoration. In its centre was the Large (Assembly) Hall, with two enfilades running from it – Darya's and Varvara's apartments, named after the prince's wife and mother-in-law. The enfilades had a very unusual decor of painted tiles. Peter the Great liked to visit this palace. It was here that he received ambassadors, held his assemblies and gave sumptuous feasts. In 1981, after a major restoration, the Menshikov Palace has become a branch of the State Hermitage Museum.

Portrait of Alexander Menshikov
Painting by an unknown artist. 1716–20

The Menshikov Palace. Architects: Domenico Fontana, Johann Georg Schädel, 1710–27

The Menshikov Palace. Barbara's apartments

*The Menshikov Palace. The Walnut Drawing-Room
(Study of Alexander Menshikov)*

A notable landmark in the panoramic view of the Vasilyevsky Island embankments is the majestic building of the Academy of Arts, or of "the three noblest arts", as it used to be said – painting, sculpture and architecture. The date of its foundation is thought to be the year 1764, when Empress Catherine the Great approved the regulations of this educational establishment. A special building for the Academy was put up according to a project by Alexander Kokorinov and Jean-Baptiste Vallin de la Mothe in 1764–88. An example of early Classicism, the building became a model for a number of large-scale public structures erected in the second half of the eighteenth century. The majestic proportions and expressive façades were combined with a comfortable arrangement of flats intended for professors' and officials, a conference hall, galleries of painting and sculpture, libraries and classrooms. In the middle of the building is a round courtyard with a circular block around it, and at the corners of the main building are four smaller courtyards, which provides the huge edifice with good lighting. The well-preserved building has been always used according to its original designation. The architectural ensemble of the Academy includes the granite landing-stage with statues of ancient Egyptian sphinxes bearing the faces of Pharaoh Amenhotep III. The landing-stage was skilfully designed by the architect Konstantin Thon in 1832–34. The sphinxes were found during excavations in Egypt and the Russian traveller Andrei Muravyev bought them at the decision of Emperor Nicholas I. These mysterious stone guards, weighing 23 tons each, are about three and a half thousand years old now.

The University Embankment. The Academy of Arts.
Architects: Jean-Baptiste Vallin de la Mothe, Alexander Kokorinov, 1764–88

The University Embankment. Landing-stage with sphinxes near
the Academy of Arts. Architect: Konstantin Thon, 1832–34

The Petrograd Side

The Peter and Paul Fortress, one of principal landmarks in St Petersburg, stands on Hare Island, or Janisaari in Finnish, probably named so because hares were abundant on this island. Peter the Great liked its favourable location and began to build the northern capital from this place. Next to the fortress, under its protection, on the neighbouring island of Koivusaari, or Birch Island, now known as the Petrograd Side, were built the first streets of the city and its first inhabitants, members of the nobility and common workmen, began to settle. The earliest square of the city, Trinity Square, with the wooden Church of the Holy Trinity, then the principal church of St Petersburg, also emerged there. In the first years of the city's existence, before the shift of its centre to Vasilyevsky Island, the buildings of the Senate, collegia, stock exchange, custom-house, printing-house and other administrative, trade and cultural establishments were located on this square. The Petrograd Side has many interesting sights for its guests: the Log Cabin of Peter the Great – the first residence of the Tsar in St Petersburg, the granite embankment adorned with exotic Chinese lions-frogs Shih-tsu, the historic cruiser Aurora, the Zoo, the Botanical Garden, a mosque, and many other landmarks. Kamennostrovsky Prospekt, running across the Petrograd Side, can be called an encyclopaedia of twentieth-century architecture. The avenue links the Petrograd Side with Stone, Yelagin and Krestovsky Islands – extremely picturesque places with architecturally remarkable suburban mansions.

View of the Peter and Paul Fortress and Hare Island from the Palace Embankment

The SS Peter and Paul Cathedral. Architect: Domenico Trezzini, 1712–33
The Boathouse. Architect: Alexander Vüst, 1761–62

he Peter and Paul Fortress is the historical centre of St Petersburg. It was built to a project by Domenico Trezzini who supervised the construction between 1703 and 1734. After his death other architects continued the construction work. In 1779–87 the walls of the citadel were clad in granite. Some structures in the fortress were built in several stages. By sad irony of fate, the fortress built as a defensive structure from outward enemies was never used for military purposes. However, it had to play the role of the Russian Bastille – the place of confinement of inner enemies, the first of which was Tsarevich Alexis, son of Peter the Great.

The fortress, which is now a museum of history and architecture, unites within its walls structures of various designation and different periods. These include mighty defensive structures at the corners of the fortress walls, casemates which served as prison cells, curtain walls, the guardhouse and the Mint. The dominant feature of the fortress area is the SS Peter and Paul Cathedral, which has remained the tallest architectural structure in St Peters-

The Peter and Paul Fortress. Monument to Peter the Great. Sculptor: Mikhail Chemiakin, 1991

*The Peter and Paul Fortress.
The Peter Gate. Architect: Domenico Trezzini,
sculptor: Hans Conrad Ossner, 1714–18*

burg: the height of its many-tiered bell-tower with a golden spire is 122.5 metres. This spire crowned with the figure of a flying angel is a well-known symbol of St Petersburg. The foundation of the stone cathedral was laid to a project by Domenico Trezzini in 1712, on the site of the original wooden one, to be completed and consecrated in 1733. The cathedral adjoins the Grand Ducal Burial Vault built in 1896–1906 to a design by David Grimm, an adherent of the "Russian style".

Near the western entrance of the cathedral is the so-called Boathouse – a pavilion used for a long time for keeping the boat of Peter the Great, the "grandfather of the Russian Fleet", used by the then young Tsar to train in navigation on the River Yauza in Moscow and on Pereyaslavl Lake. The Boathouse and some other buildings within the fortress display rich collections of the Museum of History of St Petersburg. Not far from the cathedral is a monument to Peter the Great created by the sculptor Mikhail Chemiakin. The curtain walls have several gateways, including the Peter Gate built by Domenico Trezzini in 1714–18 and serving as the main entrance to the fortress.

The Peter and Paul Fortress marked the triumph of Russia and became a symbol of the new capital establishing itself firmly on the Baltic Sea. The first main cathedral in the city, the SS Peter and Paul Cathedral retained this title until 1859 when it was replaced by St Isaac's in this role. The cathedral is unusual in many respects. It became a new word in the history of Russian religious architecture – churches had been designed in a different way before the reign of Peter the Great in old Russia. Discarding the former cross-in-square standard of churches with narrow interiors, Trezzini created a new type of church with large and tall windows, known as the "hall" church, with old captured banners adding a majestic and triumphal note to the decoration of the cathedral. The Baroque iconostasis is also shaped like a triumphal arch. It was carved by a group of Moscow craftsmen under the supervision of Ivan Zarudny to be assembled and covered with gold in the cathedral. Icons for the iconostasis were painted by M. Merkuryev and his assistants, while painted panels for the walls were executed by the best masters of the period – Georg Gsell, Andrei Matveyev and others. Next to the iconostasis, is an old carved lectern used to deliver sermons. It was from this lectern that the rebel Yemelyan Pugachev and the writer Leo Tolstoy were anathematized.

The SS Peter and Paul Cathedral. Carved wooden canopied lectern. 1732 By an unknown designer

The SS Peter and Paul Cathedral
Tomb over the burial of Peter the Great
Architect: Auguste Poirot and Andrei Gun, 1865

Carefully preserved in the cathedral were the relics of the city's royal founder: his icons and an incense-burner the Tsar himself carved on a lathe. It was here, within the yet uncompleted cathedral, that Peter the Great was buried according to his own will. Starting from Peter the Great, all the Russian Emperors and Empresses, as well as their relations, were interred in the cathedral that became the royal burial place. In 1865 the tombstones were replaced with sarcophagi of white Carrara marble adorned with precious relics and icons. The tomb of Peter the Great was decorated with a Large Gold Medal bestowed to Emperor Alexander I on the occasion of the centenary of the city. Towards the late nineteenth century there was no more room for tombs in the SS Peter and Paul Cathedral and so a special burial vault was put up in 1901–08 to the east of the cathedral for burying the members of the royal family, grand dukes and grand duchesses. Leonty Benois built the burial vault to a design by David Grimm in the Baroque style.

In 1998, on the 80th anniversary of the murder of the imperial family, Emperor Nicholas II, Empress Alexandra Fiodorovna, their children and servants were buried in the cathedral. In 1918 the last Russian monarch, who had abdicated from the throne, was shot with no trial in the Siberian city of Yekaterinburg.

The SS Peter and Paul Cathedral ▶
The nave. Iconostasis
Architect: Ivan Zarudny, 1722–26

Railing around the Log Cabin of Peter the Great. 1852

The small building known as the Log Cabin of Peter the Great, is the first house put up for the Tsar in the northern capital and the only wooden structure from that age of the city's foundation by some miracle surviving to this day. Soldiers-carpenters of the Semionovsky Regiment built the house within three days, from 24 to 26 May 1703. The modest, single-storeyed log cabin with a steep roof covered by shingles – thin edged pine plaques, became the first royal residence on the banks of the Neva. The shingles were painted to imitate tiles and the walls to look like brick masonry. A carved mortar adorned the roof and tinted wooden cannon balls were placed at the edges of the ridge. The Tsar's standard with a double-headed eagle was hoisted on a pole near it. The log cabin had neither stoves nor chimneys – the Tsar lived there only in summer. Nearby was the noisy Trinity Square where all administrative establishments of the newly built city were situated, and the mansions of dignitaries were being built next to them. The Log Cabin became the first memorial of St Petersburg – it began to be protected

Bust of Peter the Great. Sculptor: Parmen Zabello, 1875

even during the life of its owner. After the end of the Northern War Peter grew interested in the construction of more stately residences and, besides, the centre of the city tended to shift to the Admiralty Side on the opposite bank.

In 1723, when the harmful effect of the northern climate became evident, a protective pavilion was erected over the Log Cabin. The pavilion was redesigned two times in the eighteenth century. The stone structure we see today was built to a design by the architect Roman Kuzmin in 1844. In 1852 the building was surrounded with an iron fence and in 1875 a garden was laid out in front of the house. The Tsar's bronze bust by the sculptor Parmen Zabello was set up in the garden.

In 1830 the Log Cabin became a museum devoted to the memory of the founder of the city and everyday life of the early eighteenth century. The display includes Peter's personal belongings, an impression of his hand and various memorial household objects.

In the age of Peter the Great the Log Cabin stood right near the Neva. Its low swampy banks began to be strengthened from the first days of St Petersburg, since frequent floods were dangerous for the city. As a result the house turned out to be more than 70 metres from the bank, although it has never been shifted.

The Log Cabin of Peter the Great. The Study. Bureau. Russia. Early 18th century

The Log Cabin of Peter the Great. The Dining-Room

o mark the 200th anniversary of St Petersburg in 1903, the Trinity Bridge across the Neva was built and the oldest square of the city, Trinity Square, was redesigned and improved. Near its northern border the architect Alexander von Gogen erected for Mathilda Kschessinska, a dancer of the Mariinsky Theatre, a two-storeyed mansion, which is considered to be a typical example of Art Nouveau in St Petersburg. Art Nouveau came to Russia somewhat later than to Europe, but it burst into St Petersburg bringing with it a vague and changeable atmosphere of the transitional period. It seemed to emphasize the hidden and mysterious essence of the city known about long before from Pushkin and Gogol. This elegant mansion, which looks like a small palace with ingeniously designed suite of rooms, a winter garden, a grotto and a fountain, was destined to become an arena of major historical events. Mathilda Kschessinska left Russia in March 1917 and the deserted building was occupied by the committee of the Bolshevik Party for several months. Their leader Vladimir Ulyanov (Lenin) addressed the revolutionary masses from the balcony of the mansion. Today Kschessinska's former mansion and the neighbouring building house the State Museum of Russian Political History.

The cruiser *Aurora*, put on a permanent berth near the Nakhimov Naval School at the Petrovskaya Embankment of the Large Nevka, is another memorial associated with the revolutionary events. In 1956 a branch of the Naval Museum was opened at the cruiser. One of the best armour-plated cruisers of its time, built at the Admiralty wharf in St Petersburg in 1897–1903, *Aurora* took part in the famous Battle of Tsushima with the Japanese Fleet. On 25 October 1917 its forecastle cannon made a blank shot that was a signal for the attack of the Winter Palace where a session of the Provisional Government was then being held.

Mansion of the dancer Mathilda Kschessinska. Architect : Alexander von Gogen, 1904–06

The Nakhimov Naval School (the former Municipal School named after Peter the Great)
Architect: Alexander Dmitriyev, sculptor: Vasily Kuznetsov, 1909–11

The cruiser Aurora. Engineer: K. Tokarevsky, 1897–1903

The Summer Gardens

The Summer Gardens, founded simultaneously with the city, lie in the central part of the northern capital, on an island formed by the Neva, Fontanka and the Swan Canal. In 1704–05 Peter the Great himself supervised the laying out of the royal "kitchen garden" at his summer residence. The Tsar wanted to make the Summer Gardens "better than the Versailles of the French King." Plants for the garden were brought from all corners of the country and from abroad. The garden was designed in the then fashionable regular style with a strictly geometrical arrangement of its avenues, with hedges, groups of trees, busts, statues and whimsical park structures – a grotto, summer pavilions, galleries, labyrinths and trellises. The gardens that lived through several disastrous inundations suffered great damage from them: the fountains of Peter's age were destroyed in 1777 to be never restored; other structures in the gardens were also damaged. The Summer Gardens turned into a landscape park, while retaining the straight avenues, hedges alongside the Fon-tanka and some of the sculptural decor. The magnificent railing protecting the Summer Gardens on the Neva side, a work by Yury Velten and Piotr Yegorov, was erected in 1773–76. The railing on the Moika side produced after a project by Louis Charlemagne, appeared in the 1820s. While walking in the garden you should not miss a chance to visit the Summer Palace of Peter the Great, to drop into the Coffee House and the Tea House, as well as to enjoy the monument to the fable writer Ivan Krylov and many marble sculptures.

Avenue in the Summer Gardens

riginally the Summer Gardens reached the bank of the Neva – the present-day embankment was constructed in the second half of the eighteenth century. In Peter's time guests used to arrive in boats to ornate wooden galleries which served both as piers and reception rooms. It was there that Peter's famous assemblies as well as court festivities and receptions for envoys were held. Until the end of the eighteenth century the gardens were accessible only to the Tsar's closest associates. Guests walked along the straight avenues running amidst clipped shrubs and trees alternating with flowerbeds and green grass arranged in whimsical patterns. Highlights in the shady avenues were white marble statues of deities, busts of emperors and heroes and the allegorical figures of characters from Aesop's fables.

The statuary always was a pride of the Summer Gardens as it is today. In Western Europe, it was a custom to decorate gardens and parks with works of ancient sculpture and Peter shared the tastes of his age. However, sculpture was not only an element of decoration for the Tsar, who invested their use with an edifying significance. The Summer Gardens were for

Sculptural group: Cupid and Psyche. *Late 17th century*
By an unknown sculptor

Statue: Ceres. *Early 18th century*
By an unknown sculptor

Cabianca, Antonio Tarsia, Marino Gropelli and others. Peter the Great succeeded in acquiring authentic ancient works of sculpture, although their export was forbidden. 89 out of 250 pieces of marble sculpture produced by the Italian masters have reached our days. Few places in European countries have such large collections of garden sculpture.

In the nineteenth century the Summer Gardens were not as extensive and sumptuously decorated as during the age of Peter the Great, but they still remained the largest and most beautiful in the capital. During the entire May it was the favourite place of promenades of high society and in the summer, when the choice public left the city, the gardens used to be quiet and desolate. Writers, poets and composers liked to meet in the wide and shady avenues. The great poet Alexander Pushkin, who lived in Panteleimon Street nearby in 1834, often came for a stroll here.

Nowadays, inhabitants of St Petersburg rank the Summer Gardens among their most favourite places of recreation and walks. They form, together with the Summer Palace of Peter the Great, a historical museum and still gladden their guests by the unparalleled railing on the Neva side, white marble statues and the calm of its shady avenues.

Statue: Architecture. *Early 18th century*
By an unknown sculptor

him a sort of the "Academy" where Russian people were introduced to the European education. Therefore statues were arranged so that they would match one another in their subject matter and the same principle was employed in their purchases. The busts of army leaders and emperors served to extol royal power and representations of characters from ancient mythology allowed inculcating the ideas of enlightenment necessary for Russia. Thus, the statue *Architecture* commissioned by Peter the Great was associated with an important historical event – the construction of St Petersburg.

The earliest piece of sculpture in the Summer Gardens is the sculptural group *Cupid and Psyche*. It depicts the culminating episode of the myth when Psyche lit a lamp to see the face of her sleeping lover, the god of love Cupid. But on awakening he immediately left Psyche because the gods forbade her to look at him and he used to come to her only by night.

Statues might seem somewhat naive and not very skilfully made to a contemporary taste, but their value now, in the same way as before, lies primarily in their harmonious blending with the surrounding elements of the gardens.

Peter the Great bought statues or commissioned them through his agents in Italy, for Russia had no secular sculpture in his time. Venice was especially famous for its school of garden sculpture. Statues and busts for the decoration of the Summer Gardens were made by the eminent Venetian masters Pietro Baratta, Giovanni Bonazza, Francesco

The Summer Palace of Peter the Great. Architects: Domenico Trezzini, Georg Johann Mattarnovi, sculptor and architect: Andreas Schlüter, 1710–14

eter the Great, who was fond of water, always sought to settle near a river, lake or sea. So his first stone dwelling in St Petersburg, the Summer Palace, stands right on the bank of the Neva, near the place where a smaller river, then known as the Nameless Channel, flew into it. Later this river came to be called the Fontanka because it gave water for the fountains of the Summer Gardens. A small harbour was dug out on the southern side of the palace and the Tsar could descend to the boat waiting for him right from his house. The harbour has long since been filled with earth and the Summer Palace has become a museum. A small two-storeyed building reminiscent of houses of Dutch burghers of the early eighteenth century, was built in 1710–14 by Domenico Trezzini and its decoration was contributed by the well-known German architect Andreas Schlüter. The bas-reliefs produced by Schlüter for the façades and placed between the windows of the ground and first floors, feature subjects from ancient mythology celebrating the naval power of Russia and its victory over Sweden in the Northern War. The rooms of Peter the Great were on the ground floor, while Catherine and their children occupied the first floor. Both storeys had the same number and arrangement of the rooms.

The palace conveys the spirit of that time and reflects the architectural features of Peter's age conditioned by the state tasks. The ancient Russian traditions are combined here with the features of Western European fashions. The corridor, connected with all the rooms of the palace, is the only interior designed traditionally. The other rooms are located as a suite, a principle that quickly won recognition in the Russian Baroque. Now the interiors are furnished with authentic pieces from that age. The furniture, articles of carved wood and glass, precious fabrics and mirrors, ceiling paintings and beautiful pictures were all characteristic of court life in the early eighteenth century.

The Summer Palace of Peter the Great. The Bedroom of Peter the Great

*T*he St Michael (Engineers') Castle is one of the most specific architectural monuments of the late eighteenth century. It was put up and decorated for Paul within less than four years after he had become the Emperor of Russia in 1796. He decided to put up a residence for himself as a formidable castle-citadel in the centre of the capital. He chose the site where the wooden summer palace built by Rastrelli for Empress Elizabeth had stood. The construction of the castle started on 26 February 1797. In order to speed up the construction work, statues, ceiling paintings, bas-reliefs and other elements of decor were taken from the Tauride Palace and other mansions as well as from the uncompleted St Isaac's Cathedral. The construction carried out from drawings by Vasily Bazhenov was supervised by Vincenzo Brenna. The ceremony of the consecration of the building took place on 8 November 1800, the day of the Archangel Michael, whom Paul thought to be his patron, hence the name of the castle. Forty days after Paul had moved into the building conspirators strangled him in his own bedroom.

Portrait of Emperor Paul I
Painting by Stepan Shchukin. 1796–97

*View of the St Michael (Engineers')
Castle from the Summer Gardens*

View of the St Michael (Engineers') Castle from the Panteleimon Bridge ▶

*View of the Moika, Field of Mars
and barracks of the Pavlovsky Regiment*

ext to the Summer Gardens lies the Field of Mars – the largest square of St Petersburg. During the time of Peter the Great there was a marsh in this area from which the Rivers Mya and Krivusha (now the Moika and the Catherine Canal) flew out. Peter ordered to drain the marsh and had two straight canals, linking the Mya with the Neva and the Swan and Red Canals, dug along the sides. The drained expanse was used to build a palace for Catherine I, Peter's consort, and the deserted place began to be called the Tsarina's Meadow. The grounds were used for the training and parades of the Guards Regiments as early as the time of Peter the Great. On festive days popular amusements took place here accompanied by fireworks and therefore the area became also known as the Amusement Field. Later it was renamed the Field of Mars in the Western manner. The barracks of the Pavlovsky Regiment were built at the western border of the field in 1817–20 to a project by

Vasily Stasov. On 23 March 1917 the remains of the victims of the February Revolution were buried on the Field of Mars and in 1918–19 many prominent figures of the October Revolution and Civil War were interred there. At the same time the first large-scale memorial of the post-revolutionary period – the granite monument *To the Fighters of the Revolution*, was unveiled on the Field of Mars, and in 1957 an Eternal Fire was lit in the area. For nearly two centuries the Field of Mars was a dusty and negligent expanse in the centre of the city dubbed ironically the "St Petersburg Sahara". In the 1920s, a large flower parterre divided by wide avenues was laid out in the area to a project by the architect Ivan Tomin.

The Field of Mars serves as a vivid background for the monument to Alexander Suvorov unveiled during the first anniversary of his death on 5 May 1801 and created in 1799–1801 by the sculptor Mikhail Kozlovsky. The symbolic statue dedicated to the great soldier shows the Roman god of war Mars. Contemporaries regarded the monument as a symbol of the military glory of Russia.

*Suvorov Square. Monument to Alexander Suvorov. Architect: Andrei Voronikhin,
sculptors: Mikhail Kozlovsky, Fiodor Gordeyev (bas-relief), 1799–1801*

Nevsky Prospekt

Nevsky Prospekt is the main thoroughfare of St Petersburg. "There is nothing better than Nevsky Prospekt, at least in St Petersburg!" wrote Nikolai Gogol. The avenue stretches for about 4.5 kilometers and pulls together, like a bowstring, the bend formed by the Neva within the city. In the 1710s a cutting was made through the forest and the road to it from the Novgorod Highway was straightened. Monks of the Monastery of St Alexander Nevsky were building the road from opposite direction towards the Novgorod Highway. The city's central street, known before 1783 as the Nevskaya or Large Perspective, owes its name to the monastery. During the reign of Catherine the Great Nevsky Prospekt became the main street of St Petersburg. The large-scale construction of palaces, mansions, churches, trading rows and public buildings on it was in full swing. At the beginning of the nineteenth century hotels, tenement houses and banks began to appear on Nevsky Prospekt. Towards the beginning of the twentieth century the largest banks concentrated on Nevsky and it became the financial centre of Russia. The present-day appearance of the avenue is changeable and varied: eighteenth-century buildings neighbour here later structures. Numerous rivers and canals crossing Nevsky Prospekt make a promenade along it even more exciting.

Nevsky Prospekt near the Trading Arcade.
Photograph of the early 20th century

The River Moika crosses Nevsky Prospekt. On its embankment, in house No 12, is the Pushkin Memorial Flat – one of the most celebrated museums not only in St Petersburg, but in Russia as a whole and even beyond its borders. The poet settled in this mansion with his family in the autumn of 1836 and lived here the last four months of his life. Every year on 10 February (29 January Old Style), the day of Pushkin's death, lovers of poetry gather at the museum to celebrate the memory of the great poet. The commemorative meeting traditionally begins at 2:45 p.m. when the heart of Alexander Pushkin stopped beating.

The museum dedicated to the memory of the poet opened in 1925, but then it occupied only seven rooms in the house on the Moika. In 1987, in connection with the 150th anniversary of the poet's death, the entire flat has regained its original appearance. Thanks to the efforts of scholars, museum workers, architects and restorers the historical furnishings of all the rooms were re-created. Of particular value in the museum is the Pushkin Study with the poet's large library on its shelves. This room was the principal one for Pushkin in the entire house. When the poet made up his mind to move from

Portrait of the Poet Alexander Pushkin
Painting by Orest Kiprensky. 1827

The Moika Embankment. The Pushkin Memorial Flat in the Volkonsky Mansion

The Pushkin Memorial Flat. Alexander Pushkin's Study

Moscow to St Petersburg and asked his friend and publisher Piotr Pletnev to find a flat for him, he said: "It must have a separate study and I don't care about anything else." Pushkin worked in the study either early in the morning, before getting up from his sofa, or late in the evening when it became quiet in the house. On the poet's desk are books dealing with the Petrine age – during the last months of his life Pushkin worked on *The History of Peter the Great*. The draft version of the text had been ready by January 1837, but Nicholas I forbade to publish it after Pushkin's death and it was issued only a hundred years later. Besides the desk and armchairs, some other poet's personal belongings can bee seen in the room: a bronze inkpot with the small of a figure black boy, a stick with a button of Peter the Great's camisole fixed in its knob and a wooden casket. Worthy of particular attention are also Pushkin's portraits, including the last one done during his life as well as a portrait of his wife painted by Alexander Briullov. Pushkin highly valued his library that numbered about 4,500 books. It was in this room, amidst the book shelves, that he died after his duel with Georges d'Anthès.

Portrait of Natalia Pushkina
Watercolour by Alexander Briullov. 1831–32

The Kazan Cathedral (Cathedral of the Icon of Our Lady of Kazan). Architect: Andrei Voronikhin, sculptors: Ivan Martos, Ivan Prokofyev, Fiodor Gordeyev, Stepan Pimenov and others, 1801–11

Each European capital had its principal cathedral, like the famous St Peter's in Rome. At the beginning of the nineteenth century St Petersburg also provided itself with such major church building – the Kazan Cathedral put up by Andrei Voronikhin, a serf of Count Alexander Stroganov. One of the first examples of Russian Classicism, the cathedral perfectly blends with Nevsky Prospekt. The mighty Corinthian semicircular colonnade of the cathedral's northern, side façade unfolded towards the main street of the city shaping a wide square in front of it.

The main entrance to the cathedral is on the side of Kazanskaya Street and the sanctuary is directed eastwards in keeping with the Orthodox tradition. Not violating this principal canon of church building, the architect, however, constructed the cathedral looking unlike Russian churches – it has only one dome rather than usual five and is devoid of a bell-tower: its bells are placed within the wings of the colonnade, over the porticoes. The structure of the light and slender dome was wholly assembled of forged iron for the first time in the world. The cathedral is lavishly adorned with sculpture outside – relief panels featuring biblical subjects, moulded friezes and statues in niches. The cathedral completed before the Patriotic War of 1812 became a kind of war memorial. Preserved in the cathedral were French standards and keys of the cities and towns captured during the foreign campaign, as well as the baton on Napoleon's Marshal Davout. In the left chapel of the cathedral was buried the outstanding army leader Mikhail Kutuzov and in front of the building the statues of two heroes of the war against Napoleon, Mikhail Kutuzov and Barclay de Tolly, were set up.

The colonnade of the northern façade of the cathedral

The Kazan Cathedral. The communion table and tabernacle

Contemporaries were proud that the cathedral was constructed by Russian architects and builders from local materials and decorated by Russian painters and sculptors. The opening of the cathedral on the eve of the War of 1812 against Napoleon was perceived as the triumph of Russian culture. The heroic uplift of those years could be sensed in the inner decor of the cathedral: its interior looks like a majestic palatial hall with large windows divided into three parts by rows of columns of pink Finnish marble. Retained in the cathedral is the most revered icon, *Our Lady of Kazan*, known all over Russia.

The icon was brought to the northern capital in the first decade of the eighteenth century at the request of Peter the Great. Not much survives from the rich original decor of the cathedral. Paintings replaced the sumptuous sculptural decoration, which included superb examples of Russian monumental sculpture harmoniously linked with the architecture of the building. For a long time the cathedral housed the Museum of the History of Religion and Atheism, but now it has been returned to believers and religious services are performed in it.

Icon: Our Lady of Kazan. *16th century*

The Kazan Cathedral. The nave and chancel

The Catherine Canal. The Bank Bridge
Engineer: Georg Tretter, 1825–26

Nevsky Prospekt, like the entire city, owes much of its charm to rivers and canals crossing it and picturesque bridges spanning their banks. St Petersburg is sometimes called a museum of bridges – there are 350 of them in the city, perhaps more than elsewhere in the world. Made of stone, cast-iron and ferroconcrete, drawbridges, footbridges and usual structures are all beautiful and varied in their silhouettes. They lend a special fascination and romantic beauty to the northern capital.

Not far from Nevsky Prospekt there is a fine footbridge across the Catherine Canal. It is known as the Bank Bridge because it led to the State Bank (now the building houses the University of Economics and Finance). On either side of the bridge are seated griffins – lions with gilt wings – bearing lanterns over their heads and holding the chains of the bridge in their mouths.

View of the House of Books with the Catherine
Canal. Architect: Pavel Suzor, 1902–04

The Cathedral of the Resurrection, so unlike other churches in St Petersburg, is well seen from Nevsky Prospekt. Stylized in the spirit of whimsically decorated early Russian architecture, it is especially reminiscent of the Cathedral of St Basil the Blessed in Moscow. The stylizing "Russian trend" prominent in the late nineteenth century corresponded to the policy in the field of architecture carried out by the Russian Emperors Alexander II and especially Alexander III. The Cathedral of the Resurrection is an eloquent example of the Russian style. Its position at the embankment of the Catherine Canal is not accidental – it was on this spot that Ignaty Grinevitsky, a terrorist from the People's Will organization, mortally wounded the Emperor-Liberator. For this reason the cathedral is commonly known as "Our Saviour-on-the-Spilt-Blood". The place of the tragic accident is included into the inner volume of the cathedral and because of that it stands right on the bank of the canal. Inscribed under the dome of the bell-tower is a part of St Basil's prayer conveying the idea of repentance that underlies this architectural memorial.

The Resurrection Cathedral. The Crucifixion. *1907*
Mosaics on the western façade. Executed after the original by Alfred Parland

Portrait of Grand Duke
Alexander Nikolayevich
Painting by Franz Krüger.
*First quarter of
the 19th century*

The Resurrection Cathedral ("Our Saviour-on-the-Spilt-Blood") ▶
Architects: Alfred Parland, Archimandrite Ignaty (Malyshev), 1883–1907

At first, a temporary chapel was erected on the spot of the regicide and a competition for a project of the memorial cathedral was announced. The architect Alfred Parland and the Archimandrite Ignaty (Malyshev) won the competition. Legend has it that the archimandrite had a vision of the Virgin in a dream and She showed him how the cathedral should look like. The ceremony of its foundation took place in 1883 and 24 years later it was consecrated. The memorial cathedral, despite its tragic role – to preserve the memory of the murdered Emperor, has a rather festive look. Its five domes, covered with gilt sheets and varicoloured enamels, glisten with bright colours and gold in any weather. The tallest dome of the cathedral soars to the height of 81 metres. The façades of the cathedral with small columns, window surrounds, cornices and *kokoshniks* (decorative arched gables) are faced with marble, granite and bricks of various shades, while the domes of the tent-shaped roofing, porches and apses are covered with glazed varicoloured tiles. A magnificent canopy crowned by a cross made of topaz covers the spot where the Emperor's blood was shed. The canopy and icon mounts are unique examples of jewellery and stone-carving. The twenty plaques fixed on the basement bear carved inscriptions of the major events and decrees associated with the rule of Alexander II.

The fine railing, one of the most beautiful in the entire St Petersburg, highlights the passage near the cathedral skirting it in a semicircle. The railing links the cathedral into a single whole with the Mikhailovsky Garden. The elaborate figure-shaped pillars of the railing faced with decorative bricks and its whimsically curving elegant patterns in the Art Nouveau style, recalling the branches of some rare plant and intertwining into a mysterious monogram, happily combine with the outward appearance of the cathedral.

Railing of the Mikhailovsky Garden. Architect: Alfred Parland, 1907

Domes of the Resurrection Cathedral

The four porches of "Our Saviour-on-the-Spilt-Blood", the façade and interiors of the cathedral are covered with beautiful mosaics of supreme workmanship. The mosaic decoration of the cathedral is the only large collection of examples of this kind of art in Russia dating from modern times. Their overall area is about 7,000 square metres. The mosaics were created in the workshops of the Frolov Brothers after sketches by Victor Vasnetsov, Milhail Nesterov, Andrei Riabushkin and others. Most of the walls bear representations of Gospel subjects. The mosaics of the nave show the earthly life of the Saviour, the western part is devoted to the Passion, Crucifixion and Resurrection, while the eastern part features scenes after the Resurrection.

The cathedral never served as a usual parish church and an access to it was limited. It was not used for baptism, funeral or other religious services, but preaches were read in it and services in honour of the Emperor were held on the day when he was killed. After the Revolution of 1917 the cathedral became accessible to everybody and its decor was greatly damaged. The mosaic floors, which had the upper layer of marble plaques merely five millimetres thick, were nearly destroyed. In 1930 the cathedral was closed and before the war there were even intentions to demolish it. In 1956 the building was given the status of a monument of architecture and in 1970 it became a branch of the Museum of St Isaac's Cathedral.

The Resurrection Cathedral. The Eucharist, *detail of the mosaics in the main chancel. Executed after the original by Nikolai Kharlamov*

The Resurrection Cathedral. Mosaic: Sophia, the Wisdom of God. *Executed after the original by V. Beliayev*

The Resurrection Cathedral in evening illumination

The short Mikhailovskaya Street leads from the centre of Nevsky Prospekt to Arts Square where one's attention is immediately attracted by the stately Mikhailovsky Palace — the main building of the Russian Museum. The street and palace were built only in the middle of the 1820s — previously there had been a cart-track in this area with kitchen-gardens behind it. Carlo Rossi built the palace for the younger brother of Emperor Alexander I, Grand Duke Mikhail Pavlovich, hence its name, Mikhailovsky or Michael's. Contemporaries regarded this outstanding edifice designed by Rossi as "a triumph of the newest architecture" and thought it to be unique, even surpassing all other royal palaces of the continent. Rossi, a recognized master of urban ensembles, combined the palace built according to the laws of estate mansion construction, with its immediate and distant surroundings and skilfully integrated the edifice with the architectural complex of Nevsky Prospekt. The wide vista of the street affords a fine view of the palace from Nevsky Prospekt, as well as of Arts Square with a small garden in front of it. The focus of the square is the monument to Alexander Pushkin erected in the centre of the garden to a project by the sculptor Mikhail Anikushin.

The monument was unveiled in 1957, to commemorate the 150th anniversary of the great poet's birth.

The descendants of the grand duke were unable to maintain the Mikhailovsky Palace in due order and majesty and in 1895 it was purchased from them by a decree of Nicholas II for the establishment of a national museum in its interiors. In 1898 the "Imperial Museum of Russian Art Named after Alexander III" was opened in the building. The sumptuous Mikhailovsky Palace underwent drastic alterations. The original decor of the interiors suffered a particularly large damage. Merely the Main Staircase, the Hall of White Columns and some separate elements of the decor remind us of the former luxury. However, the present-day design of the building is better suited for a display of works of art. The Mikhailovsky Palace is the principal, but not the only building of the Russian Museum. In 1916, to accommodate the growing collections of the museum, the architect Sergei Ovsiannikov attached the so-called Benois Block to the main building according to a project by Leonty Benois. Today the museum's possessions include the Engineers' Castle as well as the Stroganov and Marble Palaces. The Russian Museum is deservedly called "an encyclopaedia of Russian art" — it preserves artistic values and works of all kinds of Russian fine arts from the eleventh century to the present day.

The Mikhailovsky Palace (now the Russian Museum). Southern façade. Architect: Carlo Rossi, 1819–25

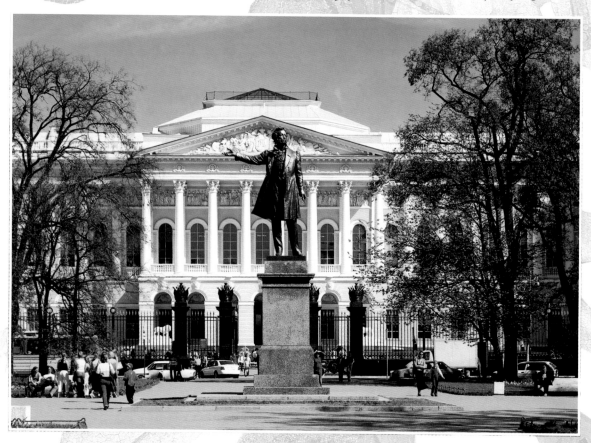

The Russian Museum. Icon: *The Archangel Gabriel (Angel with Golden Hair)*. 12th century

The display of the Russian Museum begins with Old Russian icons of the eleventh to thirteenth centuries. Worthy of particular attention among them is a small, but very beautiful icon, *Angel with Golden Hair.* The museum also boasts icons by such famous Russian masters as Andrei Rublev and Simon Ushakov. The collection of ancient Russian art owned by the Russian Museum is one of the largest in this country.

Vladimir Borovikovsky
Portrait of Maria Lopukhina. *1797*

The majestic collection of painting from the eighteenth to twentieth century is the main pride of the museum. It allows one to trace the entire development of this kind of art. The collection includes many famous works by well-known artists of all artistic trends. Portrait and history painting were particularly popular in the eighteenth century. Russia had no stable tradition of portrait painting, but during that period it began to attract a special interest despite the prejudiced opinion of the Academy treating portraiture as a lower kind of art. The flowering of portrait painting within a single century was truly amazing. Among those who largely contributed to this process were such gifted artists as Ivan Nikitin and Andrei Matveyev at the beginning of the century, Alexei Antropov in the middle, and Fiodor Rokotov, Ivan Argunov, Dmitry Levitsky and Vladimir Borovikovsky in the second half of the eighteenth century. The main reason for a rapid progress of portraiture was as usual a change in fashion – the Russian nobility, especially the courtiers, who established themselves as trendsetters, liked to commission their portraits. Admittedly, they preferred foreign masters generously paying them, so the best Russian artists began to win recognition only later.

Anton Losenko (1737–1773), a graduate of the Academy of Arts, is thought to be the first history painter in Russia. The then burgeoning Classicism in combination with the yet occurring Baroque features determined the conventional postures and gestures of characters in his

Ilya Repin. The Zaporozhye Cossacks Writing a Mocking Letter to the Turkish Sultan. *1891*

Karl Briullov. The Last Day of Pompeii. *1830–33*

pictures and their gaudiness. Karl Briullov, the most brilliant master of the Russian Academic School, was also still attached to the overworked ideas of Classicism. The most prominent exibit among his numerous subject paintings and portraits displayed in the museum is *The Last Day of Pompeii*, that made Briullov's name famous throughout Europe and won laurels at many academies for him.

The rooms of the museum show paintings by artists of the Academic School and by those active in a later period, such as Konstantin Flavitsky, Henryk Siemiradzski and others. Works by the well-known seascape painter Ivan Aivazovsky are also well represented. His famous painting *The Ninth Wave* is worthy of particular attention. Works by Alexei Venetsianov introduce to the realist trend in Russian painting, which is also represented by the canvases of Alexander Ivanov, Pavel Fedotov and other painters. Pictures by the artists of the Society for Itinerant Art Exhibitions (Peredvizhniki), such as Alexei Savrasov, Fiodor Vasilyev, Ivan Shishkin and many others, give an idea of this socially oriented trend. The rooms of the museum introduce their visitors to diverse artistic movements: the Itinerants, World of Art, Blue Rose, Jack of Diamonds, etc. Russian sculpture is also well represented in the museum – from works by Carlo Bartolomeo Rastrelli, Fedot Shubin and Mikhail Kozlovsky to pieces by contemporary sculptors.

Valentin Serov. Portrait of Count Felix Sumarokov-Elston, Later Prince Yusupov. *1903*

The Russian Museum owns works by many remarkable artists active in the Soviet period. The museum possesses a unique collection of paintings and graphic works by Pavel Filonov, one of the leaders of the Russian avant-garde in the early twentieth century. He evolved the principles of Analytical Art and offered a distinctive way of his own – the construction of form from the particular to the general. Filonov asserted the principle of an organic growth of artistic form similarly to the growth of all living things in nature. One of the fundamental ideas underlying the Analytical Method was the principle of "making". So Filonov preferred to paint large canvases with a small brush and regarded each of its touches as a "unit of action", which was both form and colour. The artist himself called to draw each atom "stubbornly and exactly" and to see in any object "the whole world of visible and invisible phenomena". He sought to express all this variety in his paintings drawing on his idea of the "seeing eye" and the "knowing eye". Filonov was an enemy of urbanism and inhumane technical civilization maiming man both physically and spiritually. He perceived the future in terms of imagery marked by primordial purity and dreamed of the world without feud and violence in which people and animals would co-exist in a harmonious unity.

Not a single leader of the Russian avant-garde could rival Filonov as regards the number of pupils. Yet nobody suffered from such cruel persecution as he did. The work of this master who spent his entire life in St Petersburg was consigned to complete oblivion. He lived like a veritable ascetic, suffered from poverty and hunger, but he never sold his paintings. Filonov died during the first months of the

Pavel Filonov. Shrovetide. 1913–14

Petrov-Vodkin. The Virgin of the Appeasement
of Cruel Hearts. *1914–15*

siege of St Petersburg. His sister, Yekaterina Glebova, saved his works, preserved them during the long years of oblivion and handed them over to the Russian Museum in 1977.

Kuzma Petrov-Vodkin (1878–1939) was one of the most interesting and original artists of the first decades of the twentieth century. His formation took place during the period when Russian society revealed for itself the Russian icon not only as a relic of ancient piety but also as an artistic phenomenon of world significance – the true value of Old Russian art was underestimated for a long time. Petrov-Vodkin evolved the original theory of painting and called it the "science of seeing". His system included the unusual method of perceiving space and its transformation on the pictorial plane as well as a specific colour range. He believed that in any kind of art one must express a connection between the depicted scene and the immense world of the universe. He invented a concrete method of rendering the feeling of

this immense world – the so-called "spherical" or 'inclined" perspective, when the horizon line was taken high and fell down towards the side parts of the painting. This method created an impression that the artist observed the earth from a high altitude evoking a "planetary" sense of the link between the everyday events depicted and the cosmic whole. The new theory of colour was also part of his artistic system. Petrov-Vodkin was convinced that paintings should be built on the combinations of a few simple colours based on red, blue and yellow. Working in this key, the artist attained the subtlest chromatic harmonies.

The theme of motherhood was one of the most important in Petrov-Vodkin work. He created a generalized image of the Russian woman – extremely vivid, attractive and singular in the fine arts of the twentieth century.

Nowadays, the Russian Museum boasts more than 400,000 exhibits, illustrating all facets of national art.

View of Nevsky Prospekt in the area of Mikhailovskaya Street and the Grand Hotel Europe
Architects: Luigi Fontana, 1870s; Fiodor Lidval, 1910–12

The Mikhailovsky Palace is the centre of the architectural complex of the Square of Arts, one of Rossi's favourite creations. The square completely befits its title – among the buildings skirting it are also the Mussorgsky Opera and Ballet Theatre and the St Petersburg State Philharmonic Society named after Dmitry Shostakovich. Since 1921 the Philharmonic Society has occupied the building of the former Club of the Gentry built by the architect Paul Jacot in 1834–39 as a commission of St Petersburg dignitaries. The beautiful white-columned hall, seating 1,500 and intended for concerts and balls, witnessed the performances of Pauline Viardot, Richard Wagner, Gustav Mahler, Richard Strauss and other great foreign masters. The premières of works by Piotr Tchaikovsky, Modest Mussorgsky, Alexander Glazunov and other national celebrities were also given here. In August 1942, in the severe conditions of besieged Leningrad, the Seventh Symphony by Shostakovich was performed here for the first time.

Also on this square, in a basement of a courtyard, was the famous artistic tavern and theatre "The Wandering Dog", the walls of which were decorated by

Grand Hotel Europe.
Restaurant Europe

Sergei Sudeikin and other fashionable artists of the early twentieth century. Anna Akhmatova, Nikolai Gumilev, Osip Mandelstam and other prominent men of letters and artistic bohemians were frequent guests at this café.

One of the most fashionable hotels in St Petersburg, Grand Hotel Europe, is located on Mikhailovskaya Street. It is associated with Fiodor Lidval, a master of the Northern Art Nouveau. He added the fourth storey and until 1914 led works on the redesigning of the hotel not violating its sumptuous if somewhat eclectic style created by the eminent architect Ludwig Fontana in the 1870s.

The improvement and decoration of Nevsky Prospekt, begun as early as the age of Peter the Great, continues to this day. Present-day builders made their contribution arranging pedestrian precincts on two small streets, Malaya Koniushennaya and Malaya Sadovaya, running from the main thoroughfare. You may walk unhurriedly along them, relax in a café, drop into a shop or view contemporary pieces of sculpture, such as *The Policeman* or *The Photographer* having nothing in common with traditional majestic monuments.

Malaya Sadovaya Street. The Photographer. *2001*

Malaya Sadovaya Street. Pedestrian precincts

The Alexandrine Theatre. Architect: Carlo Rossi, sculptors: Vasily Demuth-Malinovsky, Stepan Pimenov, 1828–32

There are several charming green areas at Nevsky Prospekt. One of them is the Catherine Garden with the monument to Catherine the Great unveiled in 1873. The majestic figure of the Empress in an ermine mantle towers on the granite pediment. She stretches her sceptre over nine bronze statues of the major state figures of her "Golden Age": Yekaterina Dashkova, President of the Russian Academy of Sciences, organizer of educational establishments Ivan Betskoi, Admiral Vasily Chichagov, Vice-Chancellor Alexander Bezborodko, the poet Gavriil Derzhavin, Generalissimo Alexander Suvorov, Field Marshal Piotr Rumiantsev and others.

The garden is situated on the square designed by Carlo Rossi. In 1828 the architect completely redesigned the section from Nevsky Prospekt to the Fontanka enlarging the edifice of the Public Library constructed in the early nineteenth century at the corner of Nevsky Prospekt and Sadovaya Street. In the depth of the square is one of the most perfect theatrical buildings in the city – the Alexandrine Theatre named after Alexandra Fiodorovna, consort of Nicholas I.

The building was constructed to Rossi's project in 1828–32. Originally the upholstery of furniture in the city's oldest theatre had the colour of cornflower, the Empress's favourite flower. The theatre struck contemporaries by the daring solution of stage engineering problems: for the first time in the history of theatre construction the roofing of the building and the ceiling over the stage and the auditorium were made in metal. The theatre was named after the square earlier known as Alexandrine Square, but in 1923 it was renamed after the famous Russian playwright Alexander Ostrovsky. The main, northern façade of the theatre with a deep loggia, six Corinthian columns and a quadriga of Apollo, the patron of arts, at its top overlooks the square. The southern façade of the theatre completes the perspective of Theatrical Street, another masterpiece of Carlo Rossi now bearing his name.

Gogol's epoch-making comedy *The Inspector General* was staged for the first time at the Alexandrine Theatre in 1836. All major plays of Russian theatrical repertory, including works by Alexander Pushkin, Alexander Griboyedov, Mikhail Lermontov and Leo Tolstoy, were also performed here. Many outstanding masters of the Russian theatre work on this stage now.

Monument to Catherine the Great. Sculptors: David Grimm, Mikhail Mikeshin, Alexander Opekushin, Mikhail Chizov, Victor Schröter, 1873

The Anichkov Bridge and Palace
Watercolour by Vasily Sadovnikov. 1840s

The Anichkov Bridge. Sculptural group: Horse Taming.
Sculptor: Peter Klodt, 1846–50

St Petersburg is a city of palaces. The imperial dinasty and the richest aristocratic families lived here from the date of its foundation. The most prominent architects built luxurious palaces for them. Most of eighteenth-century palaces, originally constructed as country estates, over the years appeared to be within the city's boundaries. The owners of estates reconstructed their palaces to give them a more up-to-date appearance. This is how the Beloselsky-Belozersky Palace emerged at the corner of Nevsky Prospekt and the Fontanka.

The architect Andrei Stakenschneider refashioned it from an estate mansion that had been built earlier and changed several owners. The architect designed the façades of the palace in the Baroque style, reminding, as it were, about Rastrelli's Stroganov Palace standing not far from it, also on Nevsky Prospekt. In 1884 the palace became the property of Alexander III's brother Prince Sergei Alexandrovich. The last owner of the palace before the Revolution of 1917 was Prince Dmitry Pavlovich. Today the Beloselsky-Belozersky Palace houses the Municipal Cultural Centre of St Petersburg.

Next to the palace is the Anichkov Bridge across the Fontanka, one of the most beautiful bridges in the city. It is named after M. Anichkov, a battalion commander, who supervised the construction of the first, wooden bridge spanning the Fontanka at Nevsky Prospekt. The bridge was reconstructed several times, but it has retained its original name. In 1841–50 it was adorned with four sculptural groups moulded and cast by Peter Klodt. They depict some moments in the taming of a wild horse by a youth.

The Anichkov Bridge.
Sculptural group: Horse Taming
Sculptor: Peter Klodt, 1846–50

The Beloselsky-Belozersky Palace.
Architect: Andrei Stakenschneider,
sculptor: David Jensen, 1846–48

The St Alexander Nevsky Monastery. The Cathedral of the Holy Trinity. Architect: Ivan Starov, 1776–90

The Monastery of St Alexander Nevsky, which gave its name to the main street of St Petersburg, lies in a picturesque place at the end of Nevsky Prospekt. It is nearly of the same age as the city itself. In 1710 Peter the Great issued a decree to start the construction of a large monastery dedicated to Prince Alexander Nevsky. The Emperor himself chose the site for it on the left bank of the Neva, near the spot where the Black River (now the River Monastyrka) empties its waters into it. Legend has it that the foundations of the monastery were laid at the site where the Novgorod prince defeated the Swedish army in 1240. In 1712 the first wooden church was built and later the construction of the entire complex of monastery buildings in brick according to a large-scale project by Domenico Trezzini began.

St Petersburg had no saints of its own and so Peter the Great ordered to bring the holy relics of St Alexander Nevsky to the newly built capital from Vladimir. On 30 August 1724 the holy relics were delivered to St Petersburg. The Russian Orthodox Church had canonized Prince Alexander Nevsky back in 1545 and thus the young city on the Neva acquired its heavenly patron and Peter the Great demonstrated the continuity of the historical tradition in Russia's struggle for the outlet to the sea. The complex of the Monastery of St Alexander Nevsky, with the Cathedral of the Holy Trinity as its compositional centre, was formed in the course of more than seventy years, but it was based on the designs created during the age of Peter the Great by the architects Domenico Trezzini and Theodor Schwertveger. The monastery complex includes eleven churches, monks' cells, various structures and several cemeteries. Many members of the royal family, statesmen, army leaders, scholars and men of letters were buried there. Nowadays, the St Alexander Nevsky Lavra is a functioning monastery of the St Petersburg Eparchy.

The St Alexander Nevsky Monastery. The north-western tower. Architect: Pietro Trezzini, 1758–70

The five domes of the Resurrection Cathedral of the Smolny (Resurrection) Convent

The Resurrection Cathedral of the Smolny (Resurrection) Convent
Architects: Bartolomeo Francesco Rastrelli, 1748–62; Yury Velten, 1762–69; Vasily Stasov, 1832–35

The complex of the Smolny Convent, a masterpiece of the Russian Baroque, is a picturesque ensemble on the left bank of the Neva. It is located on the spot where in the eighteenth century stood the modest Smolny Palace and even earlier, in Peter's age, the Tar Yard – a warehouse for boiling and keeping tar necessary for the Russian fleet – was established. Tar means *smola* in Russian, hence the common name of the Resurrection Convent founded by the pious Empress Elizabeth Petrovna on the eve of her 40th anniversary. The Empress entrusted Bartolomeo Francesco Rastrelli with the task of building the ensemble. Rastrelli, who knew the tastes of Elizabeth and her inexhaustible love for life, conceived the convent as a palace. Elizabeth wished the convent to include a five-domed Orthodox church modelled on the Cathedral of the Assumption in the Moscow Kremlin. The architect fulfilled her desire, but the domes-towers he designed adjoin the drum of the main dome. Rastrelli found a superb correlation of proportions between the domes of the cathedral and its lower mass. The principal church of the convent, the Resurrection

Cathedral, seems to be inscribed in a rectangular formed by the cells, refectory, library and four churches.

On the death of Elizabeth the construction work was suspended, and the Seven-Years' War also hindered its progress. Rastrelli's project included a 140-metre bell-tower over the entrance to the convent, but Catherine the Great, who ascended the throne soon after Elizabeth, repudiated this part of the project. She ordered to complete the construction of the convent as soon as possible and it was given to the Institute for Girls of Noble Birth – the first state educational establishment for young ladies. Giacomo Quarenghi built a special block for it in 1806–08 to the south of the complex of the convent.

So the bell-tower of the Smolny Cathedral was not built in due course and soon the Baroque ceased to be the prevailing fashion. After Rastrelli's death work on the convent complex was continued by Vasily Stasov. His decor proved to be too modest in comparison with Rastrelli's project, but the interior was still remarkable for beautiful icons, a carved lectern, gilt utensils and a crystal chancel railing. In 1923 the cathedral was closed for believers. From 1990 the building houses temporary exhibitions and is used for concerts.

The Large Neva

It was not a mere coincidence that Peter the Great liked the beautiful Neva and decided to build his "Paradise" on its banks. The Neva is a quite unusual river. For the ancient Eastern Slavs the Neva was the starting-point of Baltic trade and for the Russian lands it was nearly the only way to Europe in the course of many centuries. The Neva gave an access to the distant Volga waterway, which led to the Caucasus and Central Asia as well as opened the way to the Dnieper, "from the Varangians to the Greeks". The river is wide and deep and so navigable at its entire course. The prosperity of the new capital largely depended on the Neva, which had become the city's main thoroughfare since its foundation. It does not flood in spring and does not get shallow in summer. Its level is invariably the same regardless of heavy rains or draughts. But the residents of St Petersburg were permanently expecting ruinous calamities from it. Sometimes, as a result of powerful winds blowing from the gulf water in the Neva raises to the dangerous level of several metres. That is why even now the city's inhabitants show an interest in the changeful temper of the Neva as before. Peter the Great did not encourage the construction of bridges across the Neva – he believed that St Petersburgers should prefer boats and ships to carriages. The first bridge, mounted on pontoons, was built only after his death, in 1727. Later several other bridges linked the banks of the Neva. The Palace Bridge was the last one to be completed before the Revolution of 1917.

View of the Palace Bridge and the Kunstkammer. Architect: Lev Noskov, engineer: Andrzej Pshchenitski, 1912–16

The Trinity (St Petersburg, Suvorov, Kirov) Bridge. Architects: V. Chabrol, P. Patouillard, 1897–1903

The Trinity Bridge was opened in May 1903 during the celebration of the 300th anniversary of St Petersburg. The bridge was designed by the French Compagnie des Batignolles which won the international competition for its project. According to the contract, the bridge was built by Russian workmen under the supervision of local experts.

The first bridge across the Neva, a pontoon one, existed until 1916. Installed every year in spring, it changed its position and structure, but still was unreliable and did not match the beauty of the granite embankments. In 1916 it caught fire and its burning fragments were floating down the river. Today, only the bridge's abutments on the embankment remind us of the former structure.

The earliest permanent bridge across the Neva was built in 1850. It was named the Annunciation Bridge after the nearby square (now Labour Square) and the church on it. In 1855 it was renamed the Nicholas Bridge and since 1918 it has been known as the Lieutenant Schmidt Bridge. The seven-arched bridge rested on stone piers faced with granite. The eighth span, near the bank of Vasilyevsky Island, was overlapped by the wings of the raising sections designed in the form of metal trellis girders – structures of this kind were used for the first time in this period. In 1936–38 the bridge had a major repair and its raising section was shifted from the bank to the middle of the Neva. The present-day bridge does not look like the former one; only the fine openwork railings of cast metal remind us of its original appearance.

Half a century later the second metal drawbridge, the Liteiny Bridge, crossed the Neva. It was built in 1874–79 to a project by the engineer A. Struve. The arched structure looked like that of the Nicholas Bridge, but surpassed the latter in dimensions. The raising span with a rotating wing was arranged near the left bank. After the Liteiny Bridge had functioned for nearly ninety years it became too narrow for urban transport and inconvenient for the passage of large cargo ships. The bridge was redesigned in 1965–67, but its former railings made to a project by the architect Karl Rachau have been preserved. The Trinity Bridge was the third metal one to be built across the Neva. Its construction started in 1897. The axis of this bridge lies on the Pulkovo meridian. The entrance to the bridge from the Field of Mars is decorated with two granite obelisks. The major part of the bridge consists of five spans, their dimensions gradually growing with a fine linear rhythm towards the middle of the river. The slender silhouette of the bridge combines with its economical structure and a system of steel girders innovatory for that day. The Art Nouveau design of the bridge is a work of the French architects V. Chabrol and P. Patouillard.

The Lieutenant Schmidt (Annunciation, Nicholas) Bridge
Engineer: Stanislaw Kerbiedz, architect: Alexander Briullov, 1843–50

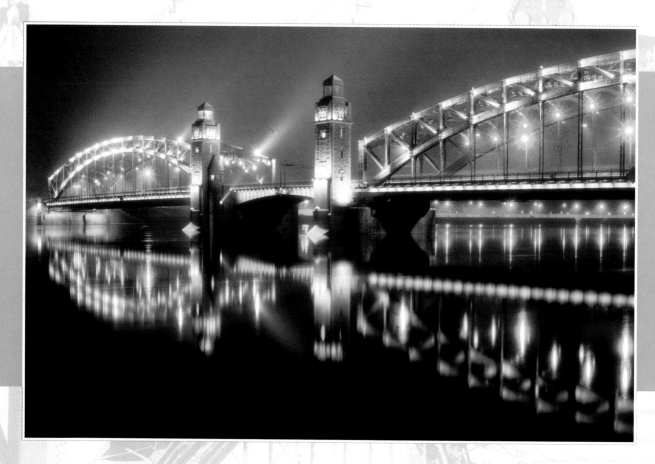

The Peter the Great (Bolsheokhtinsky) Bridge across the Neva
Architect: Vladimir Apyshkov, engineer: T. Krivoshein, 1911

The Bridge of Peter the Great (or the Bolsheokhtinsky Bridge) was constructed right near the Smolny Convent, a masterpiece of Russian Baroque architecture. The bridge crossed the Neva a little upstream from the place where the River Okhta flows into it. The Bridge of Peter the Great was constructed simultaneously with the Palace Bridge, but they are markedly different in appearance. The Palace Bridge spans the Neva in a fine area, amidst architectural landmarks, and therefore aesthetic demands were essential in its design. The Bolsheokhtinsky Bridge, on the contrary, was constructed on the then outskirts of the city and so its builders concentrated on its rational structure rather than on its architectural and artistic image. They did not even seek to harmonize it in some way with the nearby Smolny Convent. The builders of the bridge were winners of the worldwide competition for its construction organized at the beginning of the twentieth century. The work began in a festive atmosphere on 27 June 1909, the 200th anniversary of the Battle of Poltava. The unique riveted bridge is very convenient for navigation. It overwhelms us by its huge mass, immense 136-metre-long wings and granite towers soaring over the raising span. The bridge could be raised manually, too.

By night, when garlands of lights reflected in the Neva embellish the city, its illuminated bridges look especially amazing. Immobile in daytime, they are raised during the night to let ships pass upstream and downstream the Neva. Ship navigators check their routes by special lights fixed on the bridges and on the roofs of buildings lining the Neva. The raised bridges, especially in the period of the White Nights, lend an inimitable romantic quality to the northern capital. The number of bridges in the northern capital has never been the same – new bridges are being built, some old ones are replaced and some others, in a poor condition, are put under repair.

Steel arched girders of the Great Bridge

Peterhof

Peterhof or "Peter's Yard" (in 1944 renamed
Petrodvorets or "Peter's Palace")
is the capital of fountains reminiscent
of a sparkling diamond of rare beauty.
It seems to have an air of magic about it and
produces an impression of an enlivened
fairy-tale sprung, as it were, from sea-foam.
Everything here is bent to the will
of the sea, Peter's favourite element.
Peter the Great conceived to construct this
triumphal memorial and at the same time
state residence in 1705. The building
of the palace and park complex began
in the 1710s. The seaside "paradise" was
opened in a ceremonial atmosphere on 15
August 1723. It emerged on the once
desolate seashore within a surprisingly
brief period and produced an overwhelm-
ing impression on guests.
Several generations of architects, sculptors,
fountain engineers, gardeners and hydrau-
lic engineers contributed to the creation of
Peterhof's unique splendour. After the War
of 1941–45, it took another half of a
century to raise it from ruins.
The layout of Peterhof is based on the law
of symmetry, and this principle is keenly felt
in any of its sections. The main axis of
symmetry of all the structures in the Lower
Park lies at the Sea Canal running, straight
as an arrow, from the sea to the central pool
adorned with the figure of Samson.
By the sides of the canal are sparkling
fountains alternating with shady avenues.
The canal is a very complex hydrotechnical
structure. Formerly small ships could use it to
reach the Great Palace, but after the construction of the Large Pool in 1735 the canal
lost its transportation function remaining
the predominant feature of the entire Lower
Park. In 1918 the palaces of Peterhof
became state museums.

Peterhof. View of the Sea Canal and the
Alley of Fountains from the Great Cascade

Peterhof. The Great Palace and the Great Cascade. Architects: Johann Friedrich Braunstein, Jean-Baptiste Le Blond, Niccolo Michetti, 1714–24; Mikhail Zemtsov, 1730s; Bartolomeo Francesco Rastrelli, 1747–54

The rainbow of innumerable water jets makes the elegant palaces and pavilions, gardens and parks, pieces of sculpture and stone decorations at Peterhof even more charming. The focus of the majestic display is the Great Palace that dominates the natural terrace. Near the middle of the palace begins the Great Cascade, one of the most spectacular fountain structures in the world. Cut into the thickness of the natural shore ledge, the Great Cascade forms a sort of pedestal for the palace. All this majesty was created as early as the age of Peter the Great. Thanks to the subsequent efforts of architects and restorers the Peterhof ensemble has survived to the present day as an integral architectural work.

The Great Cascade celebrated the glory of Russia and Peter's victory in the Northern War, mocking in an allegorical form their enemies, the Swedes. The Large Stone Grotto, three waterfall stairways and fountains with buoyant water jets, the gilt statues of deities and heroes of antiquity, all blend into a grandiose pageant, beautiful like a fairy-tale. Through the transparent curtain of the water sliding down the cascade steps, you can discern the figures of many characters borrowed from classical mythology – Zeus-Jupiter, his beautiful consort Hera-Juno, the king of the seas Neptune with Amphitrite, Hercules, Centaur and many others.

One of the main decorations of the Great Cascade is the fountain-monument *Samson Rending Open the Jaws of the Lion*. The fountain was built to commemorate the victorious Battle of Poltava, which proved to be crucial in the course of the Northern War. The battle took place on the feast day of St Sampsonius the Hospitable. The sculptor Carlo Bartolommeo Rastrelli, creating the monument in lead to mark the 25th anniversary of the Battle of Poltava, used an allegory from the Old Testament depicting Peter as Samson defeating the Swedish lion (the lion was depicted in the state emblem of Sweden). By the late eighteenth century the soft metal had deteriorated and a new sculptural group after a model by Mikhail Kozlovsky was cast in bronze. During the War of 1941–45 the sculptural group was taken away to Germany and its destiny is unknown to this day. In 1947 Vasily Simonov and Nikolai Mikhailov cast a new bronze monument no less beautiful than the lost masterpiece.

Peterhof. Fountain: Samson Rending Open the Jaws of the Lion. *Gilt bronze Sculptors: Carlo Bartolomeo Rastrelli, 1735; Mikhail Kozlovsky, 1802*

Peterhof. The Great Palace. The Main Staircase. Architect: Bartolomeo Francesco Rastrelli, 1750s

Peterhof. The Great Palace. The Dressing Room.
Architect: Bartolomeo Francesco Rastrelli, 1750s

The Great Palace is the focal centre of the entire Peterhof complex. Johann Friedrich Braunstein and Jean-Baptiste Le Blond began building it as early as the 1710s, when the thunder of cannon in the course of the Northern War could still be heard. After the war against Sweden had been victoriously ended, Niccolo Michetti and Mikhail Zemtsov enlarged the palace and in the 1740s Bartolomeo Francesco Rastrelli rebuilt it lending to the edifice a brilliant look befitting an imperial residence. The new building stretched for nearly 300 metres, but it did not look monotonous – Rasrelli skilfully transformed it into veritable fairy-tale chambers. The luxurious palace perfectly blended with the natural surroundings revealing the perfect harmony of the "earthly and heavenly" eulogized by many poets. The subsequent alterations did not mar the artistic resplendence of the palace. Even today it appears as a stylistically integral architectural complex of the eighteenth century, although its façades and interiors illustrate various periods in history and diverse architectural styles – Baroque, Rococo and Classicism. The decor and furnishings of all the rooms were adapted to the complex ceremonies of the court etiquette and pompous theatricality of everyday life in the royal palace. Already the sumptuous three-flight Main Staircase excites a majestic mood. The Dressing Room is one of the best interiors in the northern suite. Its highlight is a masterpiece of applied art – a mirror in a silver mount sent by Louis XV to Elizabeth Petrovna as a diplomatic gift. Another valuable gift was the portrait of Elizabeth by the well-known French painter Carle Vanloo.

The elegantly trimmed rooms of the Peterhof palaces are used to display rich artistic collections of the museum.

Decorative sculpture on the Main Staircase of the Great Palace

Peterhof. View of the Great Palace and the Cascade. The Marble Bench Fountain. Architect: Andrei Stakenschneider, 1854 Sculpture: Danaid. *Copy of the original by Christian Rauch. 1854*

Peterhof. The Chessboard Hill Cascade or the Dragon Hill. Architects: Niccolo Michetti, Johann Friedrich Braunstein, 1722–30; Michail Zemtsov and others, 1731–32

Peterhof. The Neptune Fountain. *Sculptors: Christoph Richter, Georg Schweigger, E. Eusler. (Nuremberg),1652–60.* Apollo Belvedere. *Copy from an ancient original, 1970s*

eter the Great, who was fond of fountains, introduced this kind of decorative art into Russian life. Russia had not known fountains before him, although they were built in Western countries since early times. Fountains, similarly to architectural structures, were to symbolize Russia's dominance over the Baltic shores achieved as a result of the war. Fountains are the heart of Peterhof, and it is mainly to them that Peter's favourite residence owes its world renown. The fountains are especially striking for the variety of their shapes. The trick fountains, Fir-Trees, Oak and Chinese Umbrella, located on either sides of the Monplaisir Avenue, are particularly popular. They re-create the atmosphere of "water amusements" which was not rare in regular parks. Children and grown-up people rejoice alike when the fountain devices concealed in the greenery suddenly pour a spray of water on them.

The Monplaisir Avenue leads us southwards from the Palace of Monplaisir, to the largest square of the Lower Park that affords a splendid panorama of the Dragon Cascade. This is the main fountain structure in the eastern part of the Lower Park and a rare example of decorative structures dating from the first decades of the eighteenth century. It was created in 1721 after the Nystad Treaty had been concluded. Later the cascade was redesigned and the initial concept was abandoned. The three winged dragons, seemingly guarding treasures in the Upper Grotto, gush forth streams of water running down the slope for 32 metres and splashing over the pool of the grotto. Ten marble statues carved by Italian masters in the early eighteenth century flank the cascade. The boards by which water runs down from the grotto to the pool are painted to imitate a chessboard pattern and so the structure is also known as the "Chessboard Cascade".

The Neptune Fountain in the Upper Gardens is older than Peterhof for about half of a century. Produced by local sculptors in Nuremberg, it could not be installed there owing to a lack of funds. The fountain group lay in a dismantled state until Grand Duke Pavel Petrovich, the heir to the Russian throne, bought it in 1782. In 1799 the fountain was set up at Peterhof. The fountain is adorned, according to the tradition of the Petrine age, with a statue of Apollo Belvedere cast from an ancient original.

Peterhof. Palace of Monplaisir. Southern façade. Architects: Johann Braunstein,
Jean-Baptiste Le Blond, Niccolo Michetti, 1714–23

he Palace of Monplaisir ("my pleasure" in French) was Peter's favourite place at Peterhof. The name of this palace was traditional for suburban structures intended for private purposes. The palace gave its name to the entire complex in the eastern part of the Lower Park. Besides Monplaisir, it includes several gardens – tiny masterpieces of landscape gardening, a labyrinth and three flowerbeds with trick fountains. Peter himself chose the site for the palace on the shore of the Gulf of Finland, outlined the plan of the building and supervised its construction.

The southern front of the palace stretches for more than 73 metres, and its glazed galleries lend a sense of transparency and lightness to it. The unplastered walls reveal red, well fired clinker bricks; seams in the masonry are limed. This is exactly how façades in seventeenth-Dutch homes were made. That accounts for Monplaisir's former second name, the "Dutch House". The layout of its interiors, simple and elegant, also has some specific features characteristic of Dutch dwellings in that period. The Lacquer Study, the Maritime Study, the Bedroom, the Secretary's Room, the Kitchen and the Buffet are arranged in groups of three rooms around the central Hall; they are adjoined by two galleries and two small *Lusthaus* ("amusement house") pavilions. All later alterations could not erase the distinct stamp of Peter's age, which is to be found at every object. The original decor of the Hall, the main interior of Monplaisir, has happily survived to this day; its furnishings are also faithfully re-created. The room preserves unique specimens of Dutch and German furniture of the eighteenth century; the walls of the Hall are lavishly adorned with works by Dutch and Flemish painters. Peter assembled here many works of painting, which made up the first picture gallery in Russia.

The Monplaisir Garden was created as a miniature park in a regular manner. The elaborate pedestals bear pieces of sculpture restored by the sculptor A. Troupiansky after the war: *Satyr and Kid* and *Apollino* – copies from ancient originals, as well as *Bacchus* created after the original by Jacopo Sansovino.

Peterhof. Monplaisir. The Hall

Tsarskoye Selo

The town of Pushkin has a special aura about it that invariably attracts tourists. It does not lose its fascination in any season. The Catherine and Alexander Palaces, the parks and park pavilions, decorative structures and pieces of sculpture all date from distant times. At the beginning of the eighteenth century there was a farmstead, Saari mojs ("Elevated Place" in Finnish), in this area. Peter the Great presented the farmstead to his wife, Catherine I, and a small stone palace was put up for her on this plot of land. In 1725 the estate became a royal residence called Tsarskoye Selo. In 1751–56 Bartolomeo Francesco Rastrelli reconstructed for Empress Elizabeth Petrovna the modest palace of her mother into a gorgeous edifice reminiscent of a fairy-tale dream. During the reign of Catherine the Great the Church and Zubov wings were attached to the palace, the Cold Baths with the Agate Rooms, the Hanging Garden and the Cameron Gallery were built, and in 1792–1800 the Alexander Palace was put up to designs by Giacomo Quarenghi for the Empress's grandson. Closely linked with the complex of the Catherine Palace is the building of the Lyceum that opened at Tsarskoye Selo in 1811. The great Russian poet Alexander Pushkin studied in it until 1817. His name was given to the town to mark the centenary of his death. From 1949 on the building of the Lyceum functions as a state museum.

Tsarskoye Selo
The Great (Catherine) Palace. Architect:
Bartolomeo Francesco Rastrelli, 1752–56

Tsarskoye Selo. The Great Palace. The Picture Room
Architect : Bartolomeo Francesco Rastrelli, 1750s

he Catherine Palace at Tsarskoye Selo, with its façade stretching for 310 metres, was the largest building in the period of flowering of the Russian Baroque. The palace was decorated with an imposing main staircase and a long continuous suite of lavish rooms adorned with gilt carving, mirrors and amber. The architect's pride was the Great Hall occupying an area of 800 square metres. Contemporaries were amazed not so much by its unusually large size and even not by a rare abundance of gilding in the room or by its impeccable finish, as by the quantity of large windows. Glass was expensive in those days and warmth was to be saved in the cold northern climate, so rooms were usually provided with small, widely spaced windows. Rastrelli discarded this tradition and provided the hall with numerous large windows leaving only narrow piers between them with mirrors set in gilt frames. Candles lit in front of the mirrors were reflected in them and created an illusion of an endless space.

But perhaps the most striking part of the palace was the Amber Study: its walls were decorated with inlaid panels of various kinds of amber. It was even sometimes called the eighth miracle of the world. The decor of the room was created in Prussia, famous for its fine objects made of amber, the fashion for which spread all over Europe in the middle of the eighteenth century. The design of the room, as well as the idea of its creation in the palace of the King of Prussia, belonged to Andreas Schlüter, and masters of amber-working, supervised by Gottfried Turau and Gottfried Tussaud, created this unparalleled miracle of "sunny stone". On engaging Schlüter for the Russian service, Peter learned about this room from him and soon received the amber set as a diplomatic gift from Frederick William I of Prussia. The amber panels first decorated the walls in the Winter Palace and then, with royal honours, were carefully carried on hands to Tsarskoye Selo. Bartolomeo Francesco Rastrelli, who decorated the Amber Room, was short of amber for his design, and so he set Florentine amber mosaics into the decor of the walls. In 1941, when the Nazis captured Tsarskoye Selo, they send the Amber Room to Königsberg and its traces were lost. Searches of the room continue to this day. Meanwhile work on the complete re-creation of the Amber Room is under way.

Tsarskoye Selo. The Great Palace. The Amber Room
Architect Andreas Schlüter, 1710–13

Tsarskoye Selo. The Catherine Park. The Palladian (Siberian or Marble) Bridge. Architect: Vasily Neyelov, 1770–76

Tsarskoye Selo. Monument to Alexander Pushkin in the Lyceum Garden. Sculptor: Robert Bach, 1900

АЛЕКСАНДРУ СЕРГѢЕВИЧУ
ПУШКИНУ.

Pavlovsk

The complex of the Pavlovsk Palace and Park is one of the most perfect works of art in the history of Russian architecture and landscape gardening. Situated not far from the brilliant Tsarskoye Selo, Pavlovsk with its picturesque landscape park evokes romantic dreams and unhurried meditations. It was not a mere coincidence that Charles Cameron, Catherine the Great's favourite architect, who decided to implement the idea of a harmonious union of nature and architecture, began his work at Pavlovsk with the creation of a park. The construction of the palace began in 1782 and the following year already saw the completion of the main amount of work. The design of the palace is characteristic of the late eighteenth century with its prevalence of Classicism, but some specific features typical of Cameron's individual manner can also be traced. Taking into consideration the varied character of the environment – the winding Slavianka River with the whimsical outlines of its banks as well as the alternation of hills and valleys – Cameron designed all the façades of the Great Palace in a different way. The palace looks like a beautiful country-seat from the Slavianka, while its other, south-eastern aspect is that of a stately edifice befitting the royal residence. The Pavlovsk Park, the largest and probably the most picturesque in Europe, is dominated by unassuming yet charming northern scenery embellished with pavilions, sculpture, bridges and cascades. The names of alleys and walks in the park are full of mystery and enchantment: the Mushroom Walk, the Green Woman Alley, the Brave Fellow Path, etc. Maria Fiodorovna arranged strolls and amusements for her guests here.

View of the Grand Palace from the Triple Lime Avenue. Architects: Charles Cameron, 1782–86; Vincenzo Brenna, 1796–99

Monument to Paul I. 1872
Copy from the original by Ivan Vitali

avlovsk stands somewhat apart among the suburban palace and park ensembles of St Petersburg. It emerged later than other residences and its emotional atmosphere is quite different. Pavlovsk was founded in 1777, the year when Catherine the Great presented the village of Pavlovskoye to her son, Tsesarevich Pavel Petrovich, and Grand Duchess Maria Fiodorovna to mark the birth of their first son, the future Emperor Alexander I. Pavel Petrovich allowed his consort to dispose of the estate completely at her convenience, and so the history of Pavlovsk is closely associated with the memory of Maria Feodorovna. After the death of Paul I, between 1801 and 1828, the Dowager Empress was the legal owner of Pavlovsk and she made a lot to transform it into a veritable masterpiece of Russian architecture. The garden of Pavlovsk became one of the best landscape gardens in the world. Charles Cameron created there a harmonious complex made up of the palace that consisted of eight blocks having three hundred rooms, the park and various park pavilions. 600 hectares of woodland were refashioned into a beautiful park in the English style that grew fashionable in that period. The focus of the ensemble was the palace in the Palladian manner reminiscent of Italian villas and Russian country estates alike. The palace, standing at the top of a gently sloping hill on the bank of the picturesque Slavianka River provides a beautiful sight from a distance.

In the time of Maria Fiodorovna, Pavlovsk was the most famous suburban residence of St Petersburg. Its renown was based not only on the architectural and natural splendours, but also on the literary salon where the best writers of the period recited their works, as well as on educational and charitable establishments. Grand Duke Mikhail Pavlovich, the son of Paul I, who owned Pavlovsk after the Dowager Empress, refashioned it into a military town. The grand duke had no children and so after his death the suburban settlement came into the possession of the descendants of Grand Duke Konstantin Nikolayevich, the grandson of Maria Fiodorovna.

When the first railway linked Pavlovsk with St Petersburg in 1838, the concert hall at the Pavlovsk Vauxhall became a centre of musical life in the capital.

In 1917 Pavlovsk was converted into a museum of art and history. Destroyed during the war and restored to its former appearance, it serves as a museum to this day.

Pavlovsk. The Great Palace. The Grecian Hall. Architects: Vincenzo Brenna, 1789; Andrei Voronikhin, 1803–04

◀ *Pavlovsk. View of the Great Palace from the Centaur Bridge. Architects: Charles Cameron, 1782–86; Vincenzo Brenna, 1796–99. The Centaur Bridge. Architects: Charles Cameron, 1799*

Charles Cameron dreamed of transforming the Pavlovsk Palace into a temple of ancient art and it really became the "abode of the Muses and graces". Thus, the lightest and most spatial interior, the Grecian Hall, completing the middle suite of the rooms in the palace was, according to the architect's concept, to remind of an ancient temple. A row of columns runs along the perimeter of the hall as in the peristyle – the inner courtyard in a Greek dwelling house. Statues of Greek deities are plaster casts from ancient examples. The marble chandeliers in the shape of ancient lamps suspended from gilt bronze chains between the columns is another feature adding to the hall's affinity with the decor of ancient interiors. It is noteworthy that the decorative colonnade does not support the ceiling – the columns are hollow inside and are suspended from the ceiling on anchor hooks. In keeping with the old tradition, the Grecian Hall is used for concerts of classical music.

The Italian Hall, the palace's compositional centre located under the dome, is reminiscent of the Pantheon, the temple of all Roman gods. In the niches, on marble pedestals, are statues made after Greek originals. Using the techniques employed by ancient architects, Cameron emphasized the articulation of the hall into storeys. Light falling through the glazed dome onto the circle of the marble floor reflects the star patterns of its slabs.

In the park, Cameron created many magnificent pavilions, subtly blending the architecture with the environment. That is why all the fronts of the palace are designed in a different way. The first structures built by Cameron in the park were the Temple of Friendship and the Apollo Colonnade. The Temple of Friendship became a symbol of Pavlovsk. Among those who transformed Pavlovsk was Pietro Gonzaga, a decorator from Italy infatuated with Russian northern nature. He revealed himself an unrivalled master of "creating charm and magic" and was at his best in the field of "green architecture" – he created the Valley of Pools, the Red Valley and other picturesque areas.

After Cameron, the most famous masters of the times built and improved the palace and park complex at Pavlovsk. Among them were the architects Vincenzo Brenna, Giacomo Quarenghi and Carlo Rossi; the decorator Pietro Gonzago; the painters Andrei Martynov, Giovanni Scotti and Jacob Mettenleiter; the sculptors Fiodor Gordeyev, Ivan Martos, Mikhail Kozlovsky and others.

Pavlovsk. The Temple of Friendship. Architect: Charles Cameron, 1780–82

Pavlovsk. The Great Palace. The Italian Hall
Architects: Vincenzo Brenna, 1786; Andrei Voronikhin, 1803–04

Санкт-Петербург
и пригороды

Альбом (на английском языке)

Издательство «Альфа-Колор», Санкт-Петербург
Тел./Факс (812) 326-8384 E-mail: alfac@mail.wplus.net